CALIFORNIA PRISON PHOTOS

Eric "Superman" Sturgess

AF883710

Rose Of Sharon
PUBLISHING

COPYRIGHT © 2025
ERIC "SUPERMAN" STURGESS
CALIFORNIA PRISON PHOTOS
All rights reserved.

No part of this publication may be reproduced, distributed, or transmitted in any form or by any means, including photocopying, recording, or other electronic or mechanical methods, without the prior written permission of the author, except in the case of brief quotations embodied in critical reviews and certa other non-commercial uses permitted by copyright law.

ERIC "SUPERMAN" STURGESS

Printed Worldwide
First Printing 2025
First Edition 2025

10 9 8 7 6 5 4 3 2 1

Rose of Sharon Publishing books may be ordered through booksellers or by contacti

Rose Of Sharon Publishing

roseofsharonpublishing.com
P.O. Box 186
Floresville, Texas 78114

Scripture quotations are taken from the New King James
Version. Copyright © 1982 by Thomas Nelson, Inc. Used by permission.
All rights reserved.

ISBN: 978-1-970335-08-8 Paperback

Dedication

This book is a heartfelt dedication to the men in the California Department of Corrections and Rehabilitation, as well as those in prisons across America, who are striving to improve themselves and reunite with their loved ones. Within the confines of those prison walls, many men have been blessed with remarkable talents, and they take great pride in their creations and the stories they have to share. This humble book serves as a platform for their voices to be heard.

I have taken it upon myself to write numerous letters of support for resentencing and parole board hearings on behalf of my incarcerated friends in the California Department of Corrections and Rehabilitation. I am fully committed to assisting in their release, and these letters of support play a crucial role in that endeavor.

"The Lord has given them special skills as engravers, designers, embroiderers in blue, purple, and scarlet thread on fine linen cloth, and weavers. They excel as craftsmen and as designers," Exodus 35:35.

God bless you,
Eric "Superman" Sturgess
Psalm 91

Preface

Growing up in the 1970s and 1980s, Polaroid pictures were a common sight. I was always fascinated by them and how the picture slowly appeared over time. People would swing the photo back and forth like a hand fan to supposedly make the image appear quicker.

I have been collecting Polaroid pictures of convicts in the California Department of Corrections and Rehabilitation for several years now. They are rare and hard to find after all these years. The 1990s were the last decade when Polaroid pictures were commonly used in California state prisons.

These photos are a snapshot of time that captures these men doing their best to survive behind those cold prison walls. These photos and the people in them deserve to be seen by others and their lives not forgotten in the dustbins of history. It just reminds us how fleeting our lives are. Nobody is guaranteed tomorrow, and our youth quickly fades to old age if we are blessed to live that long.

God bless you
Eric Sturgess
Romans 10:9-13

Table of Contents

Dedication....3
Preface....4
Introduction....6
Photographs....8
About the Author....34
Other Books....37

Introduction

The Polaroid camera was never meant to be an archive of prison life. It was marketed as instant fun — snapshots of birthdays, vacations, and family gatherings. But inside California's prisons, the same instant film became something different. For many incarcerated men, a Polaroid was the only way to send a face home, the only tangible evidence that they were still alive behind the walls.

These images were not taken by professional photographers or staged for history books. They were created in visiting rooms, in yards, or against cinderblock walls with nothing but fluorescent light overhead. A few might show smiles, carefully pressed shirts, or arm-in-arm poses with loved ones. Others reveal the tension of survival — tattoos, hardened stares, and the weight of years still to be served. Each photo carries the marks of its environment: the faded color, the worn corners, the roughness of time.

California's prison system in the late twentieth century was notorious. Places like San Quentin, Folsom, Tracy, and Soledad earned reputations for violence and overcrowding, becoming known as gladiator schools where survival meant toughness. For those living inside, a camera was rare, and a Polaroid became both a lifeline and a shield. To mail a photo home was to remind family that you still existed. To keep one tucked in a book or on a cell wall was to hold on to identity in a place designed to strip it away.

These Polaroids show us more than uniforms and tattoos; they reveal the human face of incarceration. A man might project pride, defiance, or humor in front of the lens, but behind that single frozen frame is a story we cannot fully see — the circumstances that led him inside, the years endured, the family waiting outside, the dreams long abandoned or still clung to in secret.

This collection does not claim to tell the whole truth of prison life. No single image can. What it does is capture moments otherwise lost — faces and fragments that remind us that history is not only written in official records, but also in the small, fragile keepsakes that survive against the odds.

These Polaroids are artifacts of a hidden world, documents of resilience and confinement, and evidence of how human beings find ways to be remembered, even in the harshest places.

To look at them is to confront both the distance and the closeness of prison life. The distance lies in the razor wire, the walls, and the label of "inmate." The closeness lies in the eyes, in the hands folded or fists clenched, in the attempt to hold dignity in a place designed to break it. The instant camera may have been simple, but in these pictures, it became something profound: a tool of memory, survival, and truth.

The use of Polaroid cameras in California prisons peaked between the 1970s and 1990s, when film was cheap, instant photography was widely available, and prison regulations were looser about what could pass in and out of visiting rooms. By the early 2000s, digital security measures, policy shifts, and the decline of Polaroid itself ended the practice. What remains today are these fragile photographs — snapshots that outlasted their era, offering us a rare and unfiltered glimpse into prison life during one of California's most turbulent decades of incarceration.

Photographs

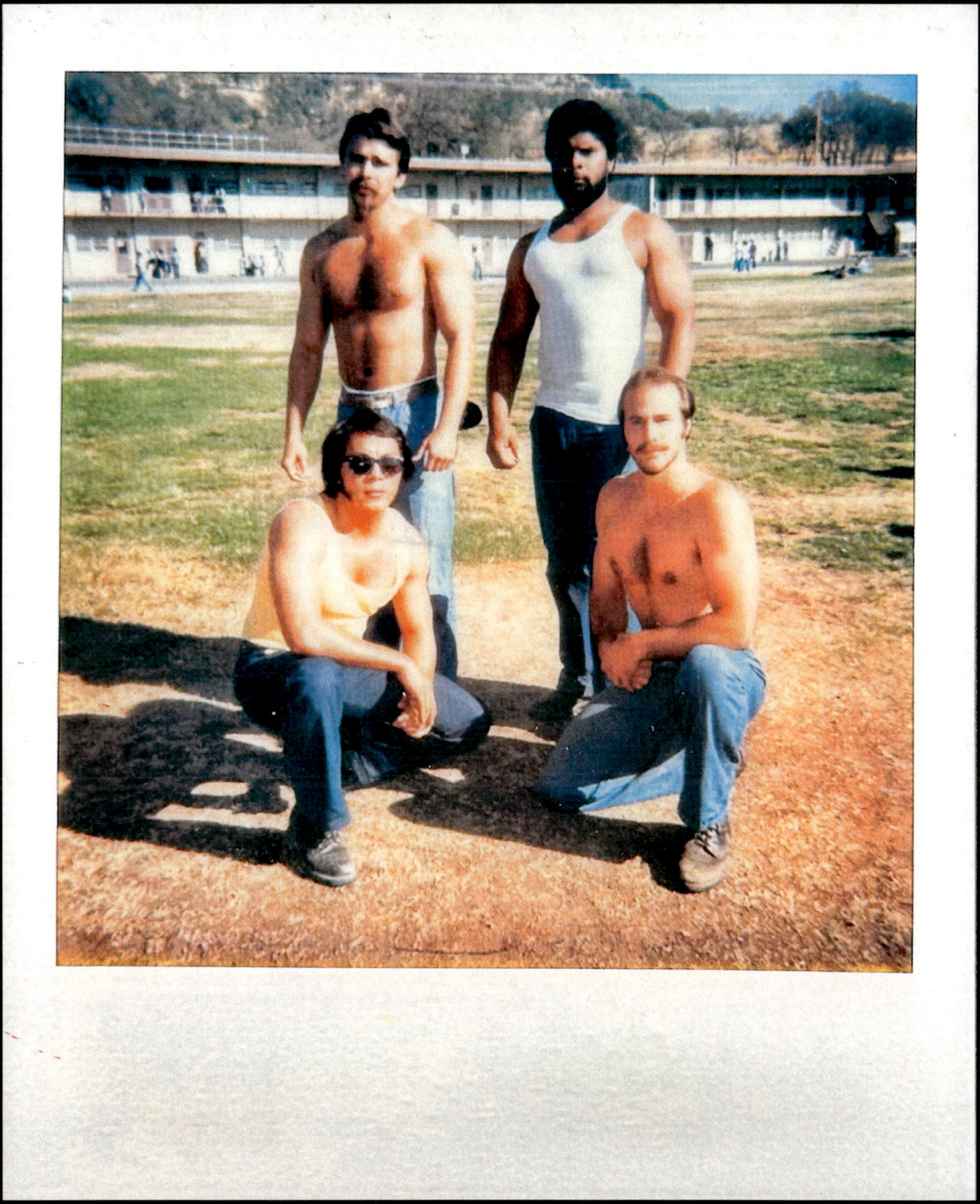

This photo was taken at Sierra Conservation Center State Prison (Jamestown) in the mid-1990s. Pictured is a group of Peckerwoods (Woods); Peckerwood is a term for "Solid" or "Regular" White convicts. The group of Peckerwoods on the prison yard is called the "Woodpile."

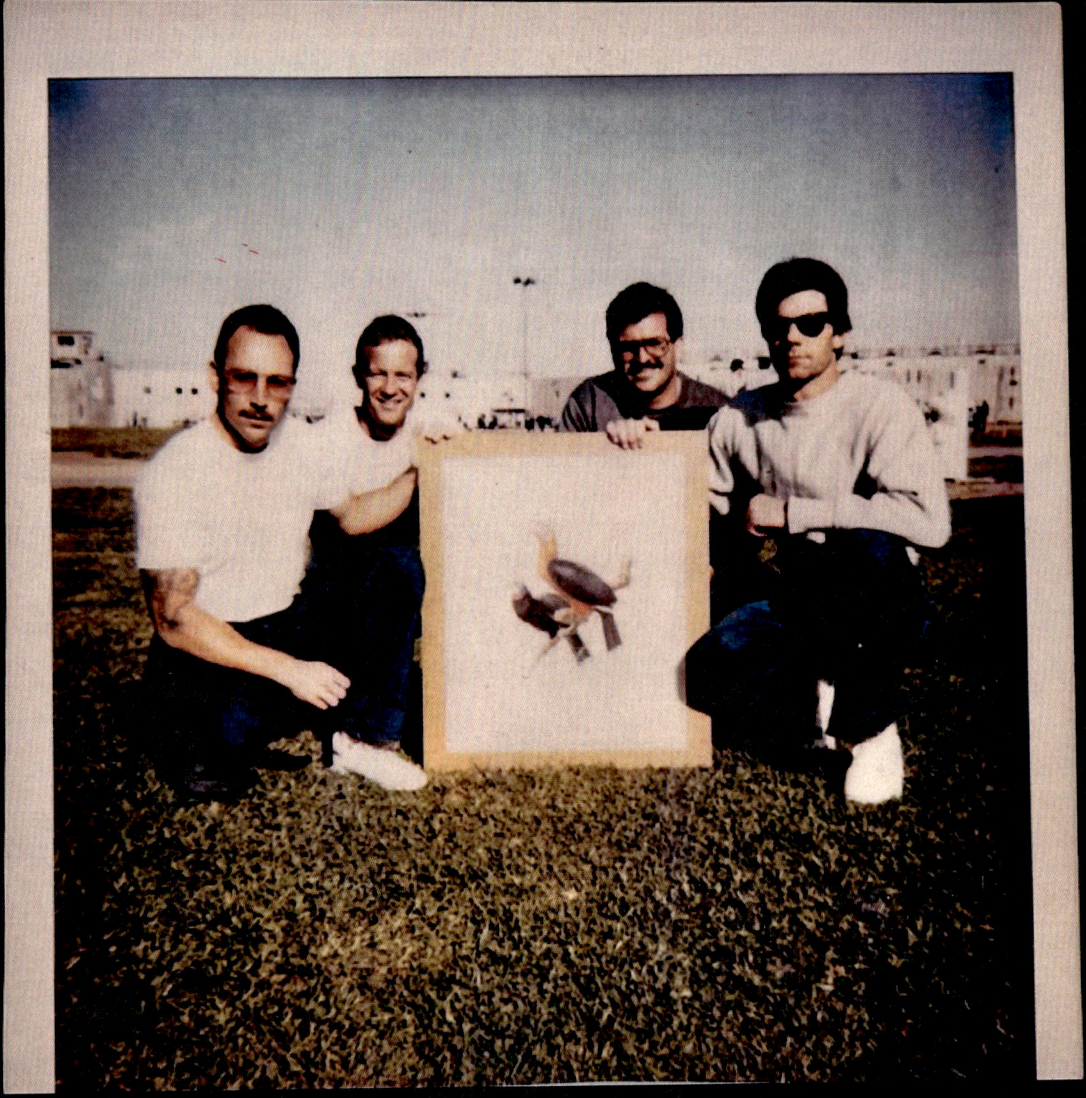

This photo was taken in the early 1990s, and it pictures a group of Peckerwoods (also known as Woods). Woods are what affiliated White convicts are called in the California Department of Corrections and Rehabilitation. They are holding a picture that one of them drew.

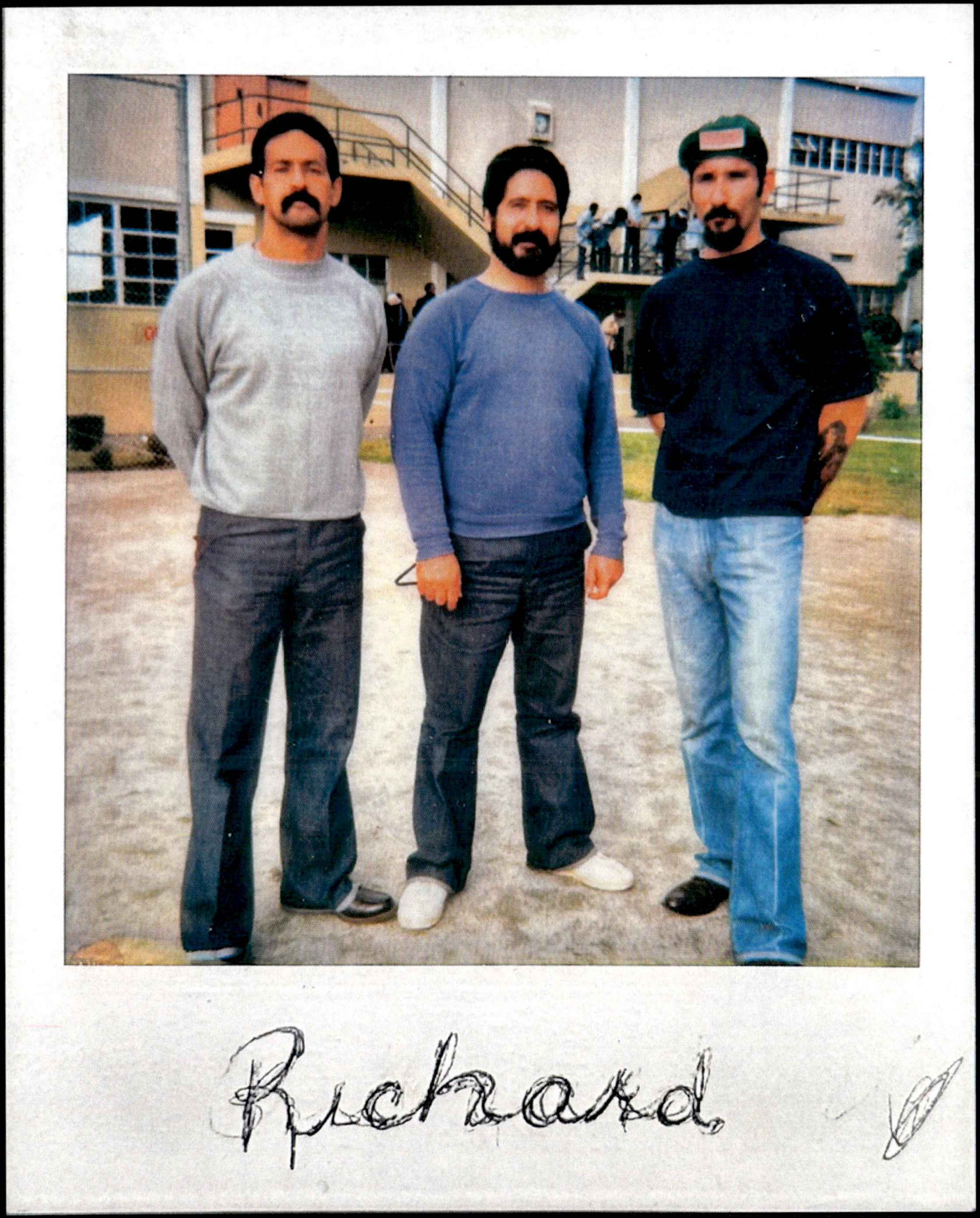

This photo was taken in the early 1990s on a low-level "Soft" California prison yard. Doing time on a soft yard is much more comfortable for inmates who previously did time on Level III and IV yards. Level II yards were nicknamed "Lifer Graveyards" because they were filled with "Lifers" whose "Points" dropped over the years.

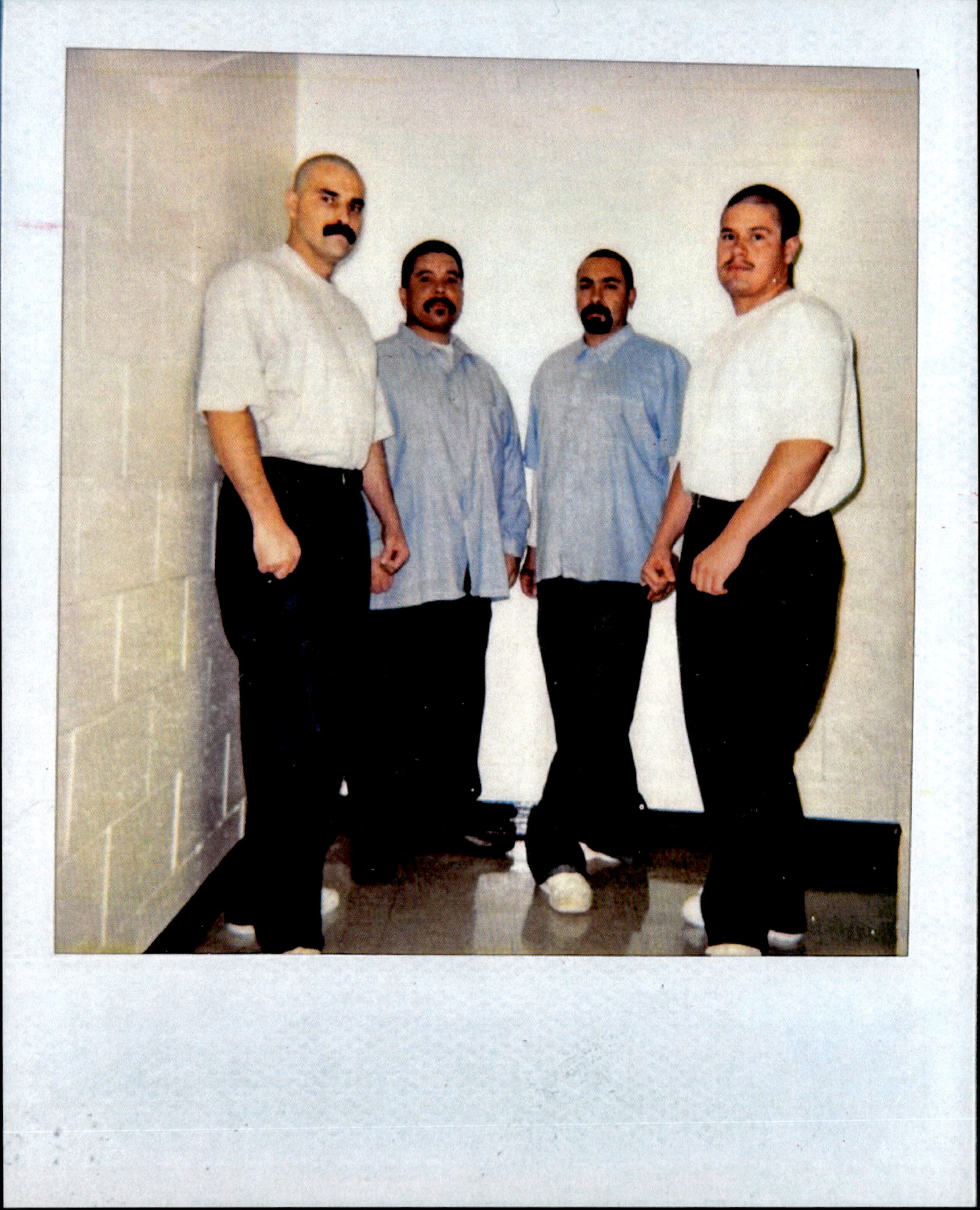

This photo of these four Southsiders was taken in the mid-1990s at an unknown California state prison. Three of the inmates pictured have the classic California gangster stance with their feet positioned in that awkward style.

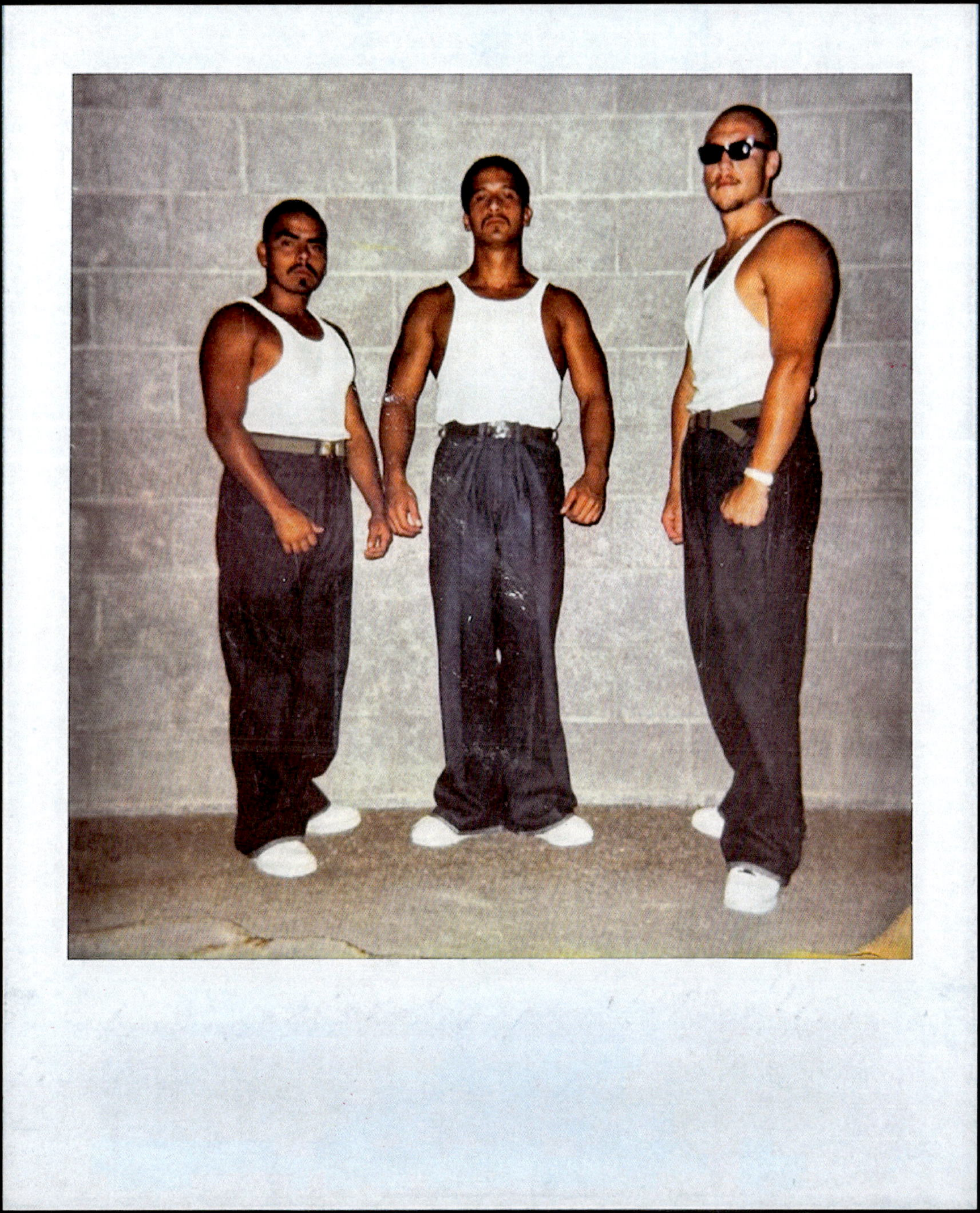

This photo was taken in the mid-1990s at Calipatria State Prison. Calipat at this time was a Level IV maximum security prison. Calipat was a notoriously violent prison that was always "Kicking Off." On June 5, 1995, five Crips rushed into the Program Office at Calipat and poked eight officers with shanks.

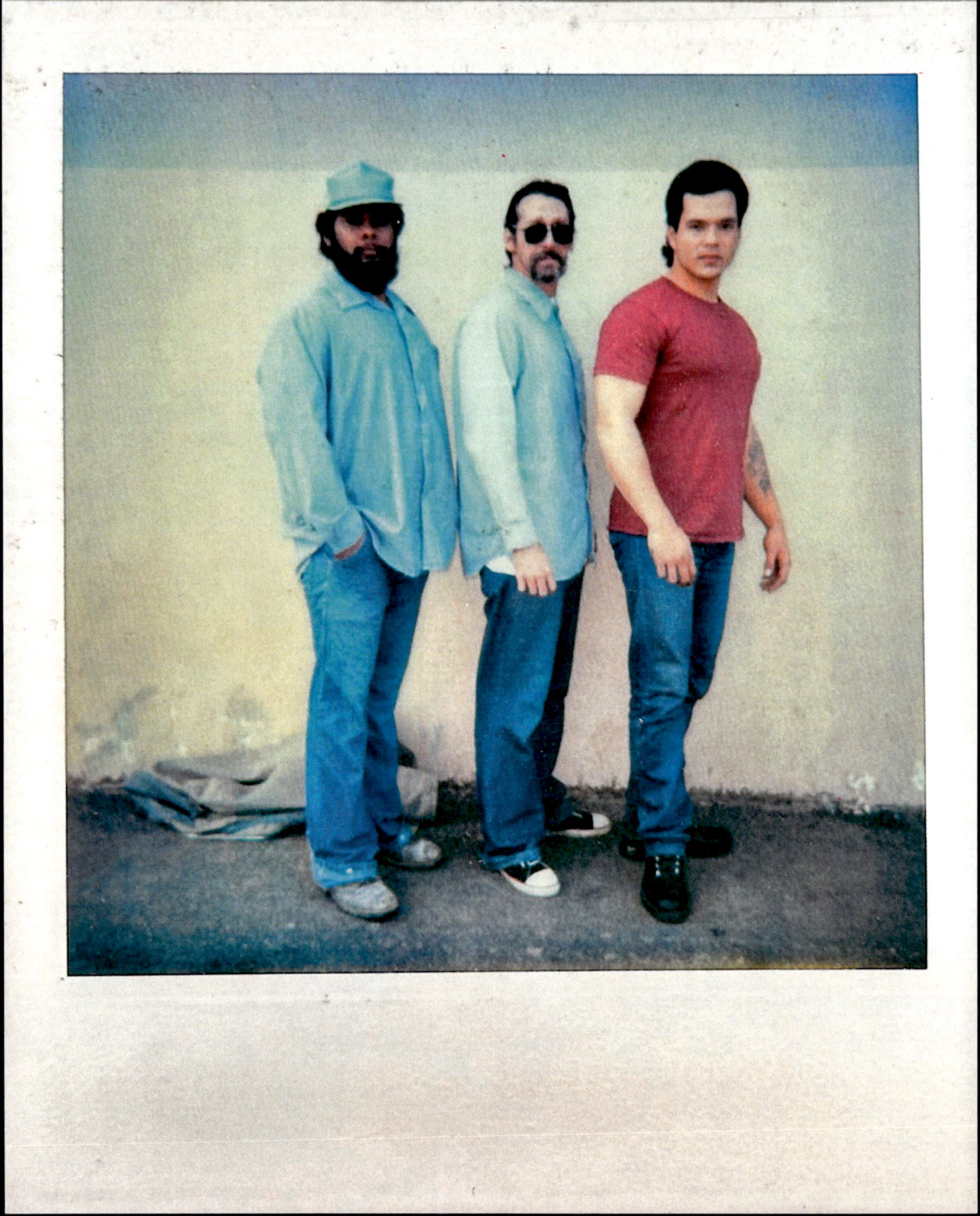

is photo was taken at Sierra Conservation Center State Prison (Jamestown) in the early 990s. Pictured is a group of Peckerwoods (Woods) standing by a concrete wall in the prison yard at Jamestown Prison.

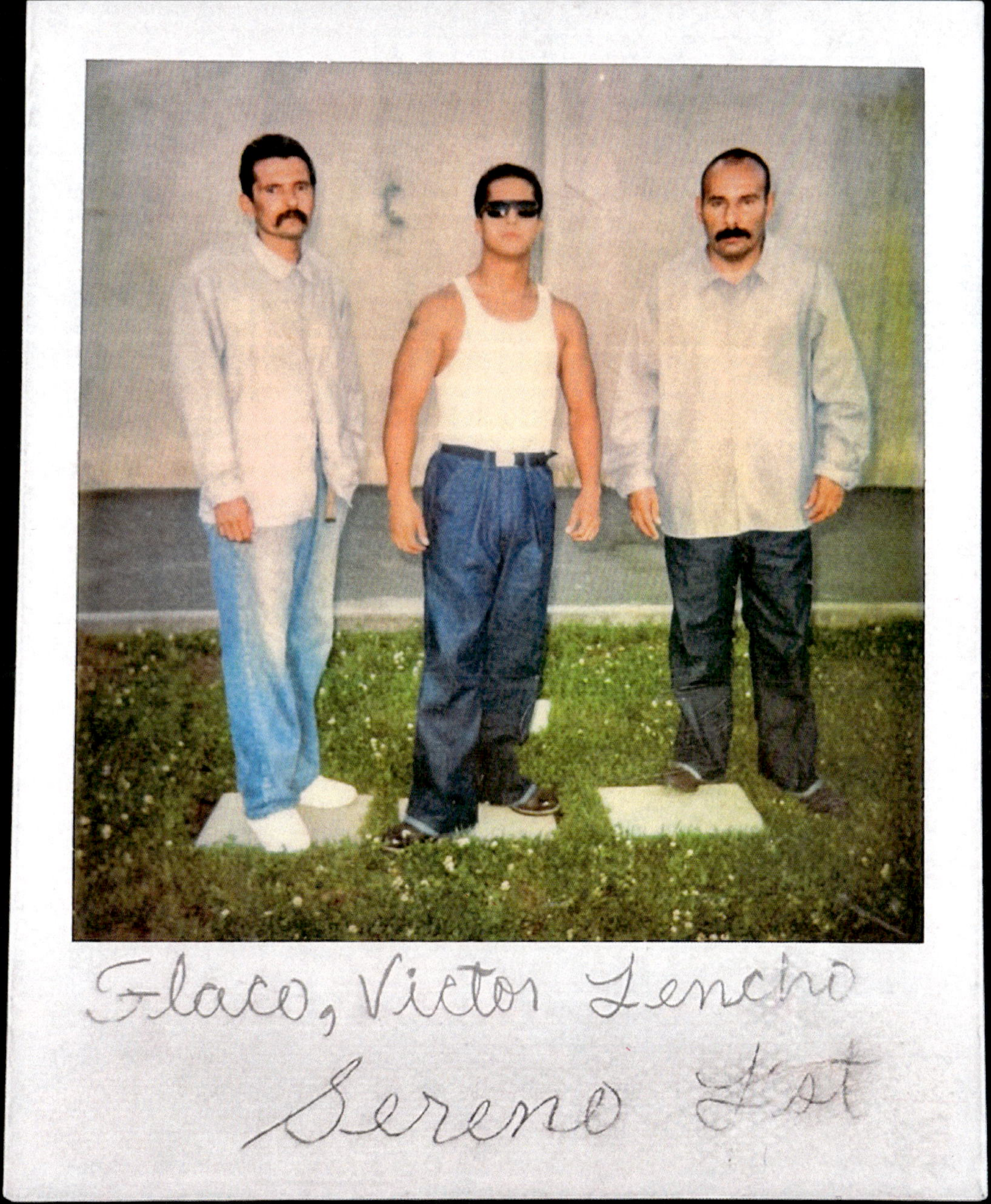

This photo was taken in the mid-1990s at an unknown California state prison. The dude in the middle has his "Mad Doggers" on, and his shoes have a really nice shine. He was definitely "Lowriding" on the yard that day. Lowriding on the yard means he was showing off.

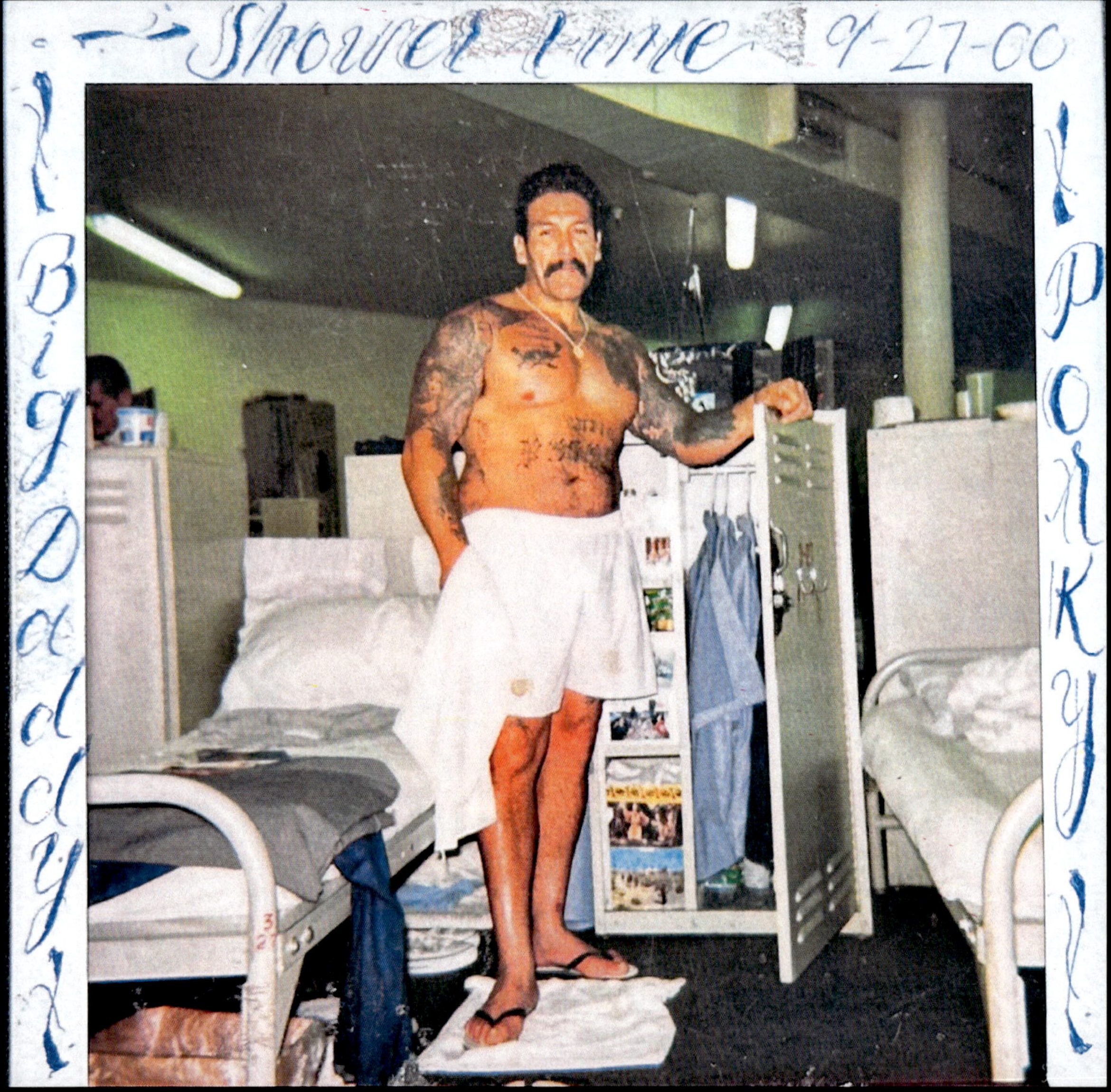

This photo depicts an inmate in an unknown California prison, taken on September 27, 2000. He is wearing his shower shoes after just getting out of the shower. He is assigned to a dorm, which is different from cell living. I never liked working in dorms, and I preferred housing units with cells.

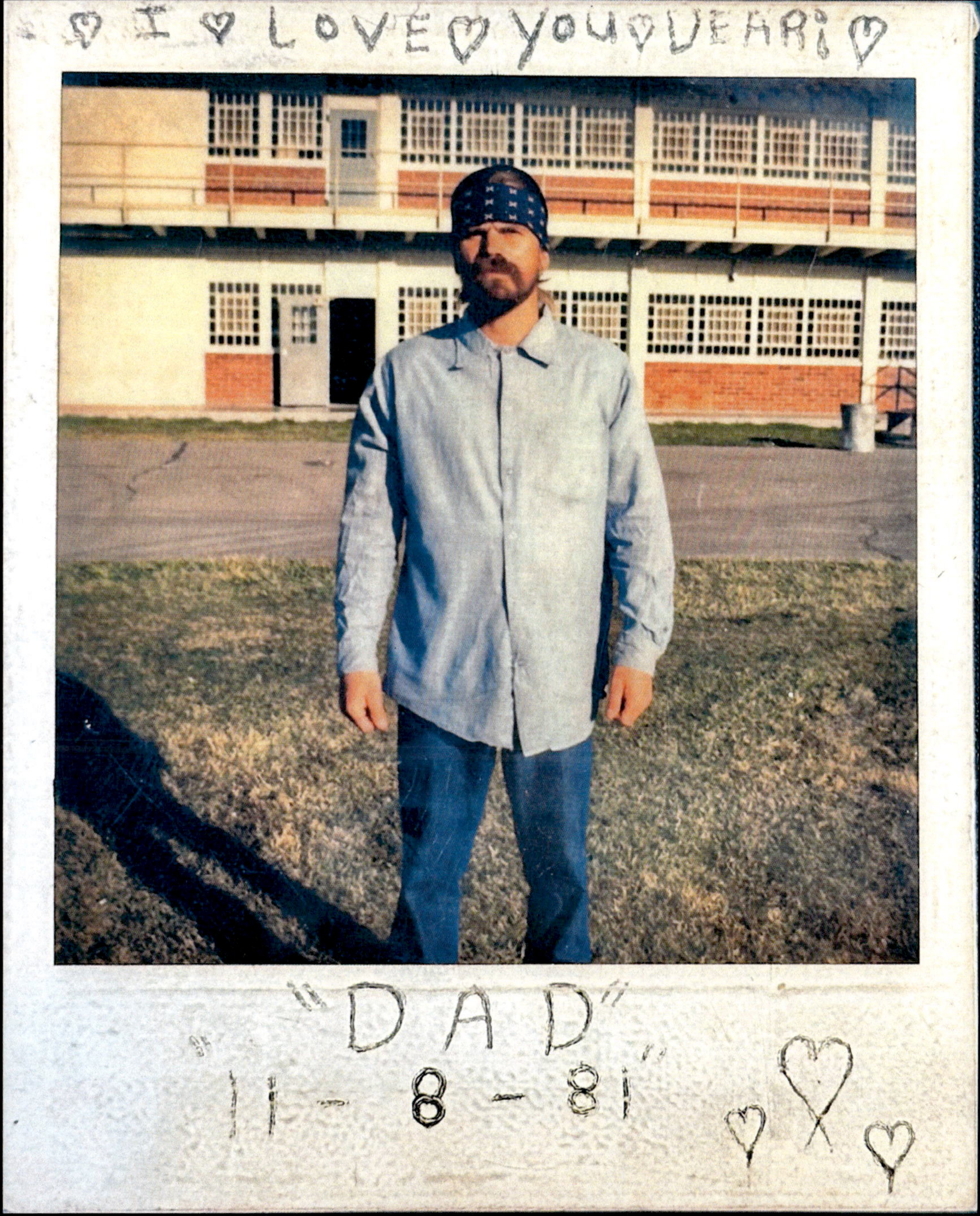

This picture depicts a White convict at Susanville State Prison, taken on November 8, 1981. The writing on this Polaroid is a sad reminder of all the years missed by children and loved ones by those men who are stuck behind those prison walls. Time continues to pass by inmates while the lives of their loved ones are moving forward without them.

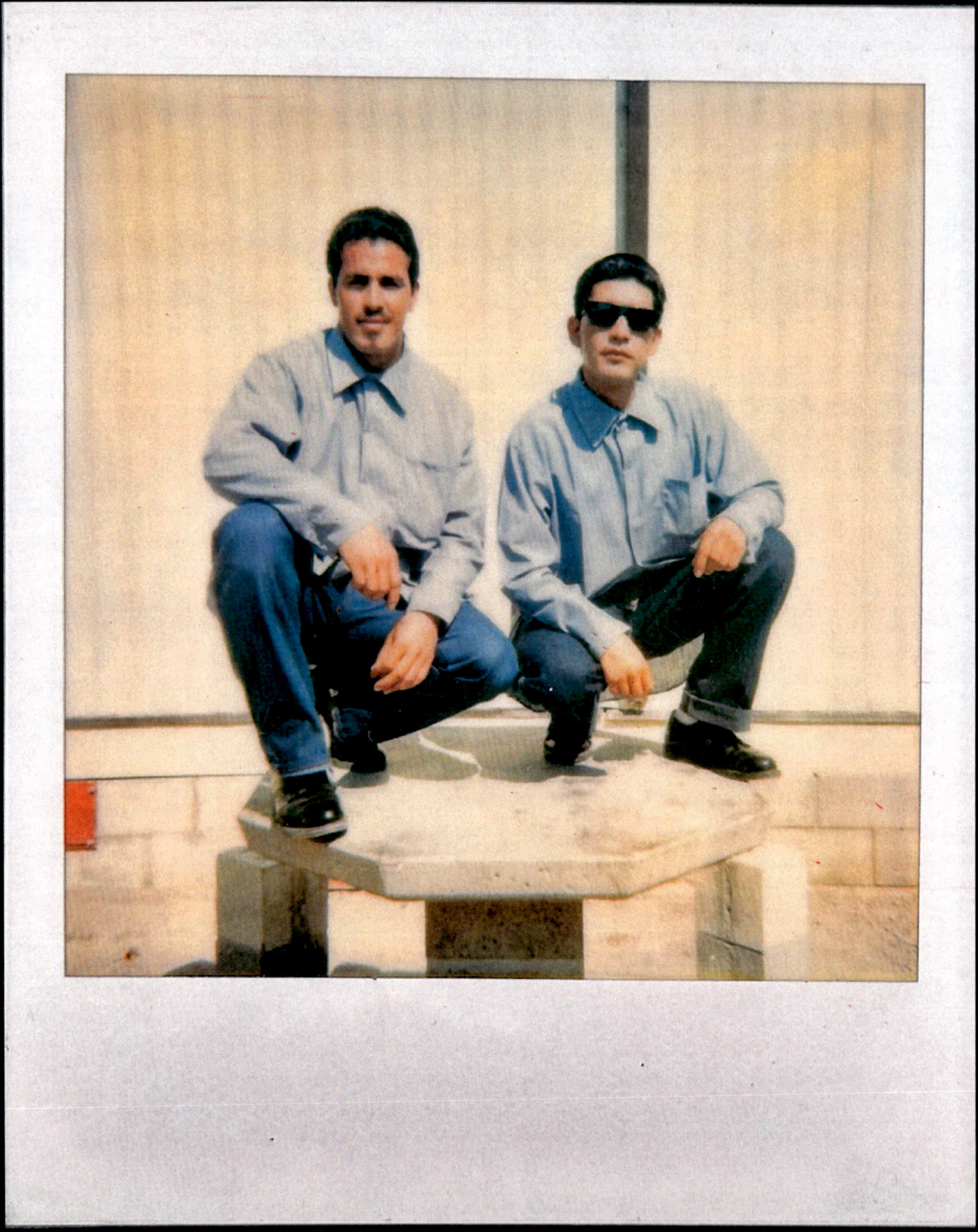

This picture was taken in the early 1990s at an unknown California state prison. This photo interested me, and I texted it to my "Lifer" friend who is incarcerated in a California prison. I wanted to know which prison it was taken at, but after he asked around the yard, he didn't get an answer.

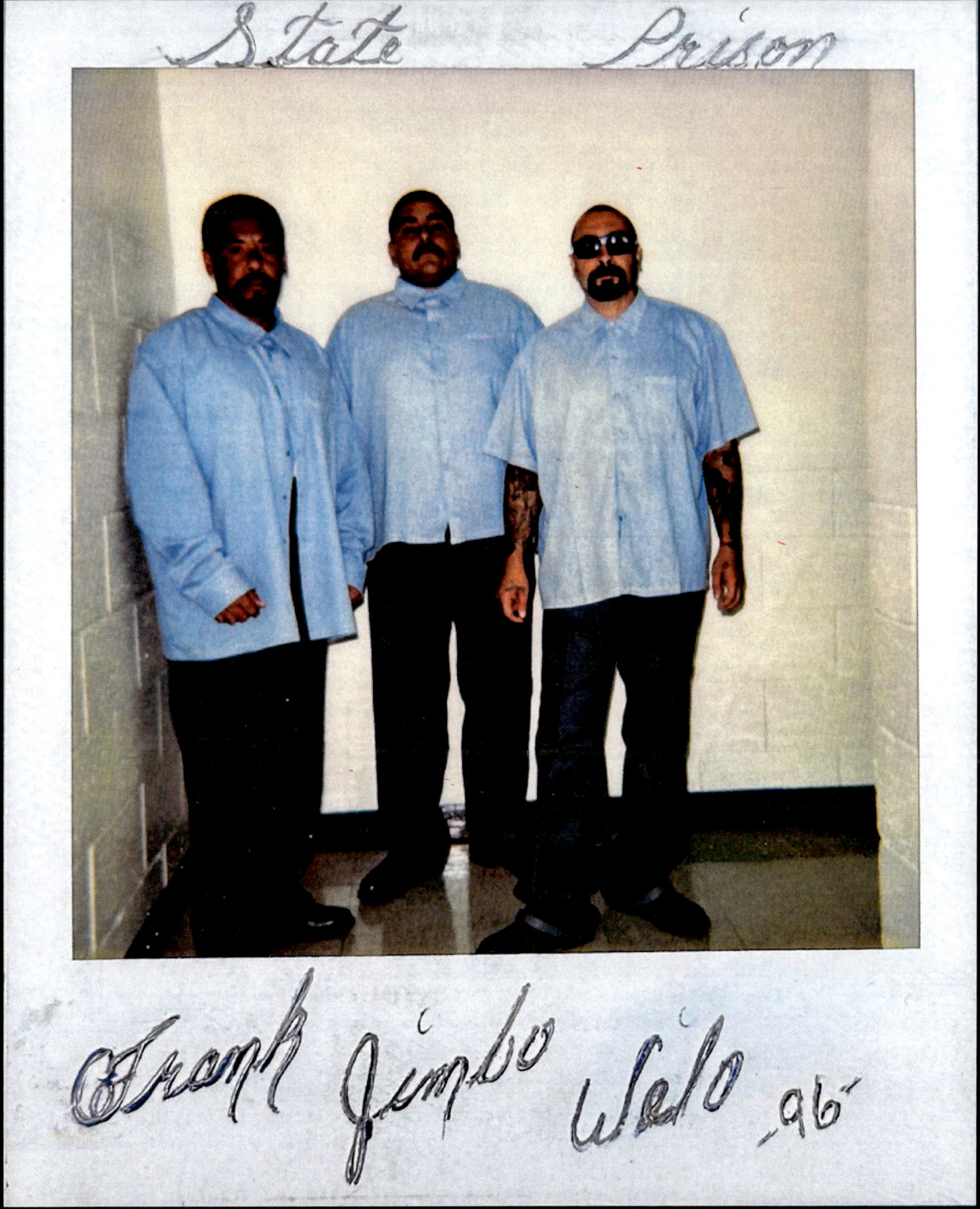

This photo was taken in 1996 at an unknown California state prison. Prison is the same boring program every day, with short periods of intense violence that break the monotony. Most of the time, you can feel the tension in the air as the yard gets silent and people group up before things "Jump Off." There is nothing like it in the world; I will never forget my years in prison.

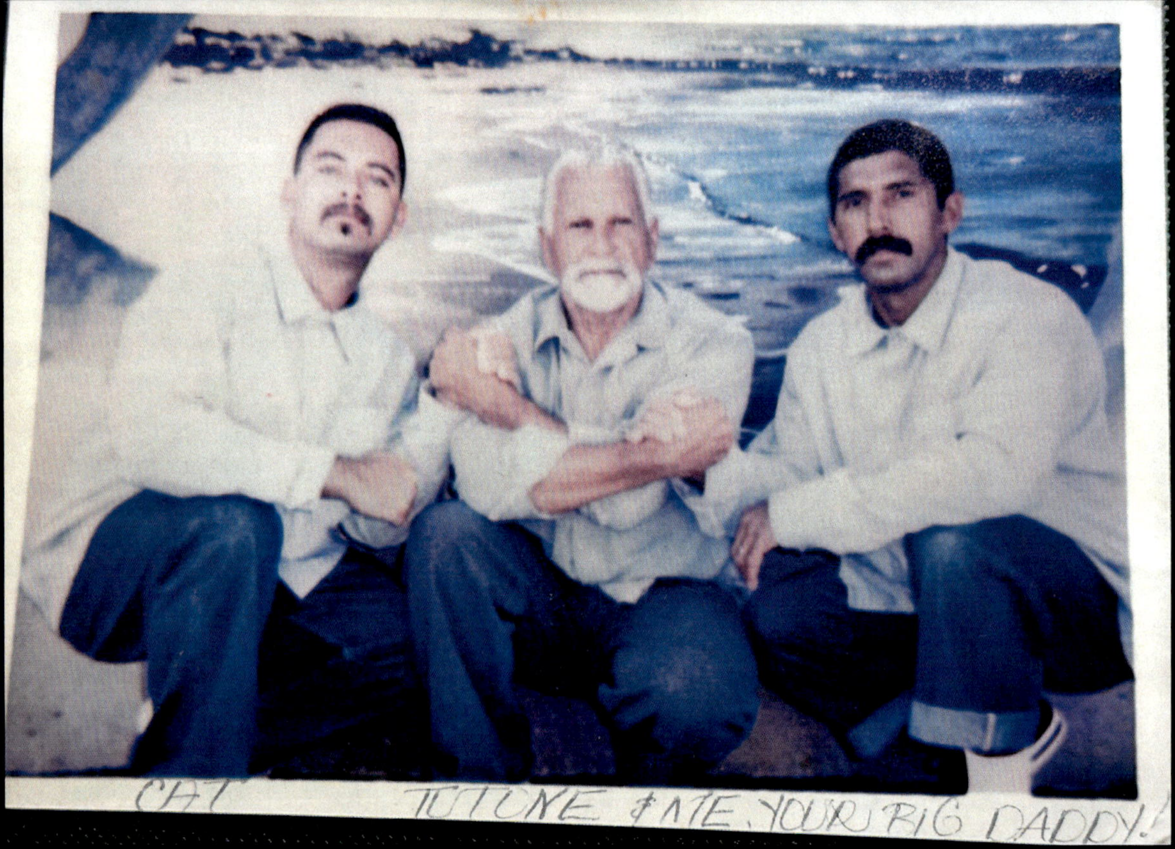

This photo, taken in the early 1990s, depicts three Southsiders on an unknown California prison yard. Several prisons back then had large murals painted on the walls by inmate artists, and they would take pictures like these in front of them. I text a couple of artist inmates who painted murals on the walls of their yards.

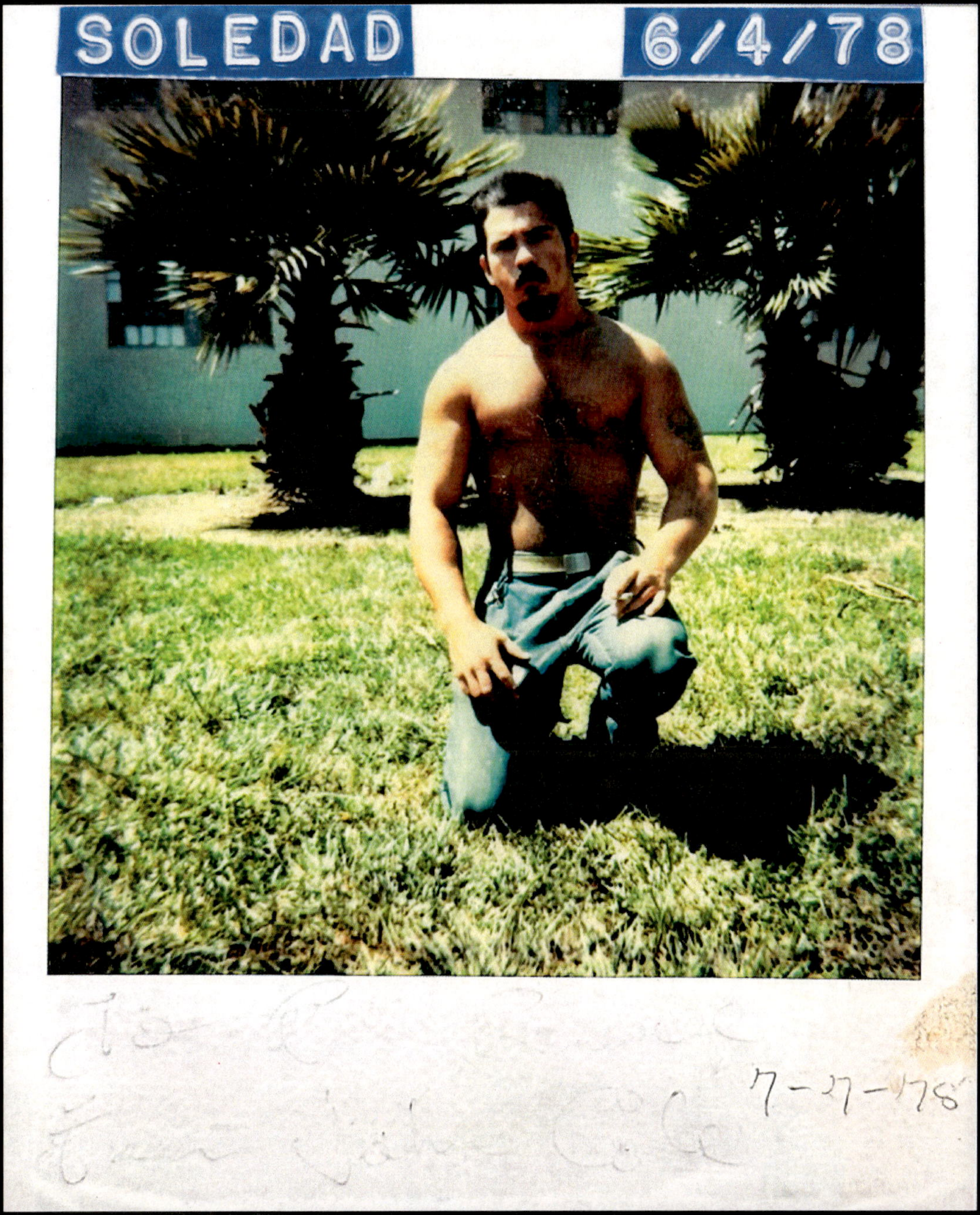

This photo, taken on June 4, 1978, at Soledad State Prison, shows an inmate kneeling on the prison yard in front of some palm trees. Soledad has one of the most storied histories of all California state prisons. The only prisons with richer and longer histories are Old Folsom, San Quentin, and Tracy.

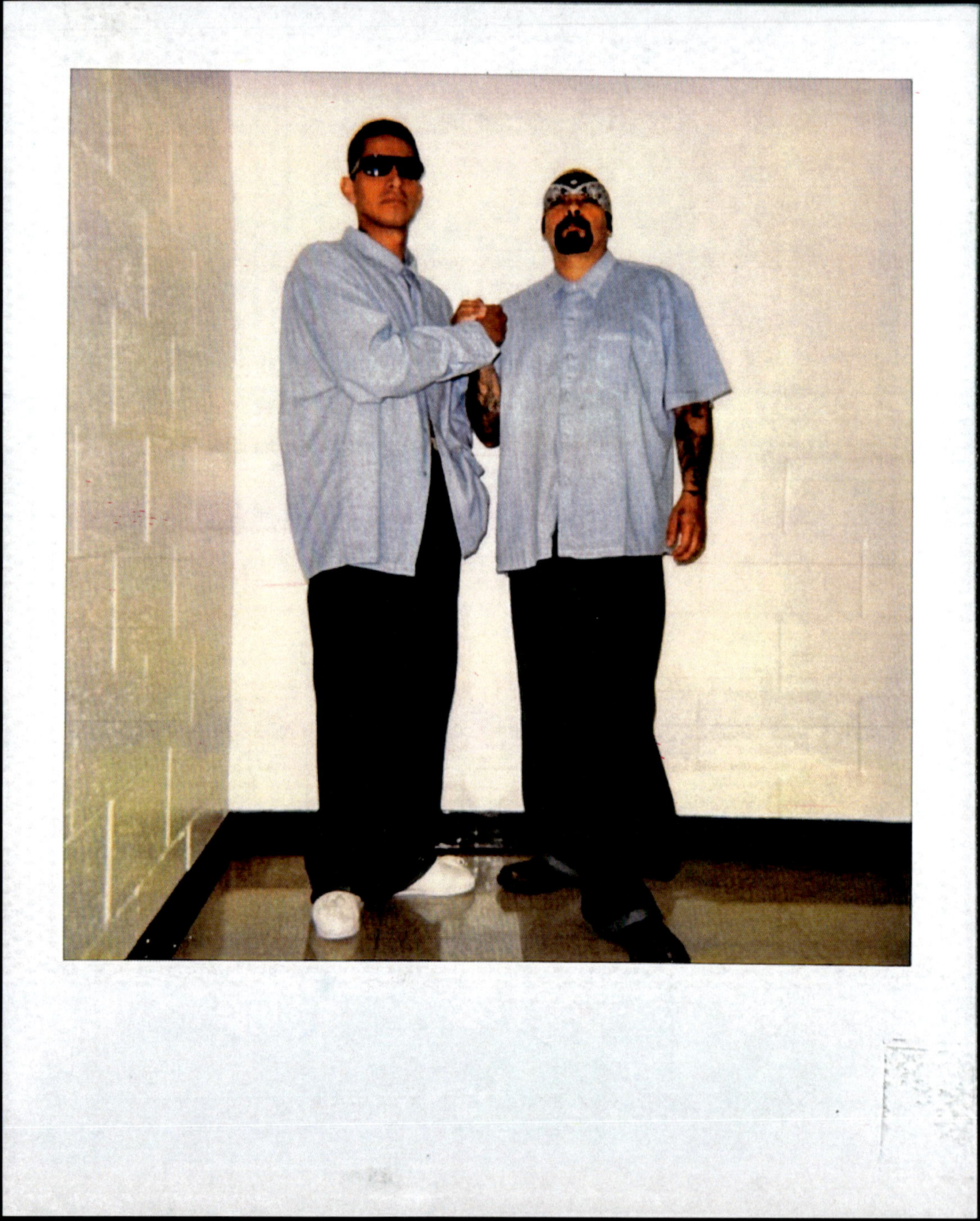

This photo was taken in 1996 at an unknown California state prison. Respect means everything in prison. You never let another man disrespect you in any way whatsoever. Your word is all you have in prison; a man is only as good as his word. Those are just some of the things I learned during my years walking the line in the penitentiary.

NCCN Guidelines for Patients®

The essential guide for people facing cancer.

Based on care recommendations from leading cancer experts.

Explains high-quality cancer care provided at state-of-the-art cancer centers.

Reviewed and revised every year.

Did you know that top cancer centers across the United States work together to improve cancer care? This alliance of leading cancer centers is called the National Comprehensive Cancer Network® (NCCN®).

Because cancer care is always evolving, NCCN develops and frequently updates evidence-based cancer care recommendations used by health care providers worldwide. These recommendations are known as the NCCN Clinical Practice Guidelines in Oncology (NCCN Guidelines®).

The NCCN Guidelines for Patients plainly explain these expert recommendations, so you can talk with your care team about the best care for you.

These NCCN Guidelines for Patients are based on the NCCN Guidelines® for Breast Cancer, Version 2.2026 — February 27, 2026.

View the NCCN Guidelines for Patients free online: NCCN.org/patientguidelines

Find an NCCN Cancer Center near you: NCCN.org/cancercenters

Learn how the NCCN Guidelines for Patients are developed: NCCN.org/patient-guidelines-process

Connect with us

@NCCNorg @NCCNVideo NCCN @NCCNorg

Supporters

NCCN Guidelines for Patients are supported by funding from the NCCN Foundation®

NCCN Foundation gratefully acknowledges the following corporate supporters for helping to make available these NCCN Guidelines for Patients: AstraZeneca; Daiichi Sankyo; Genentech, Inc.; and Novartis Pharmaceuticals Corporation.

NCCN independently adapts, updates, and hosts the NCCN Guidelines for Patients. Our corporate supporters do not participate in the development of the NCCN Guidelines for Patients and are not responsible for the content and recommendations contained therein.

To make a gift, visit NCCNFoundation.org/Donate

To learn more, visit online NCCN.org/patientguidelines or email PatientGuidelines@NCCN.org

Made in United States
North Haven, CT
05 November 2026

21765359R00040

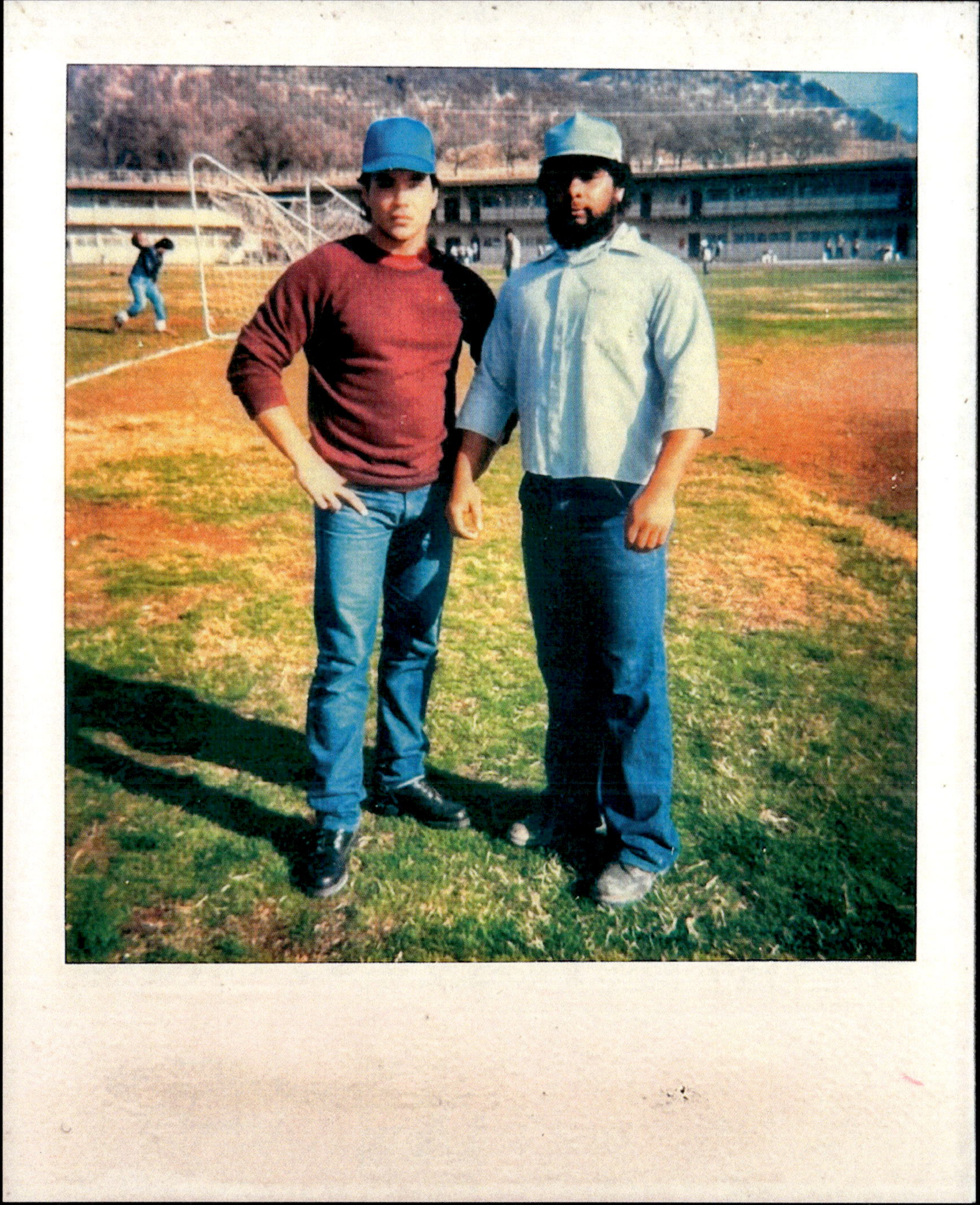

This photo was taken at Sierra Conservation Center State Prison (Jamestown) in the early 1990s. When we were being trained at Jamestown while in the academy, we wore our brown academy uniforms. Every day when we walked on the yard, the inmates would yell, “Where is my package?” In our brown uniforms, we looked like UPS workers.

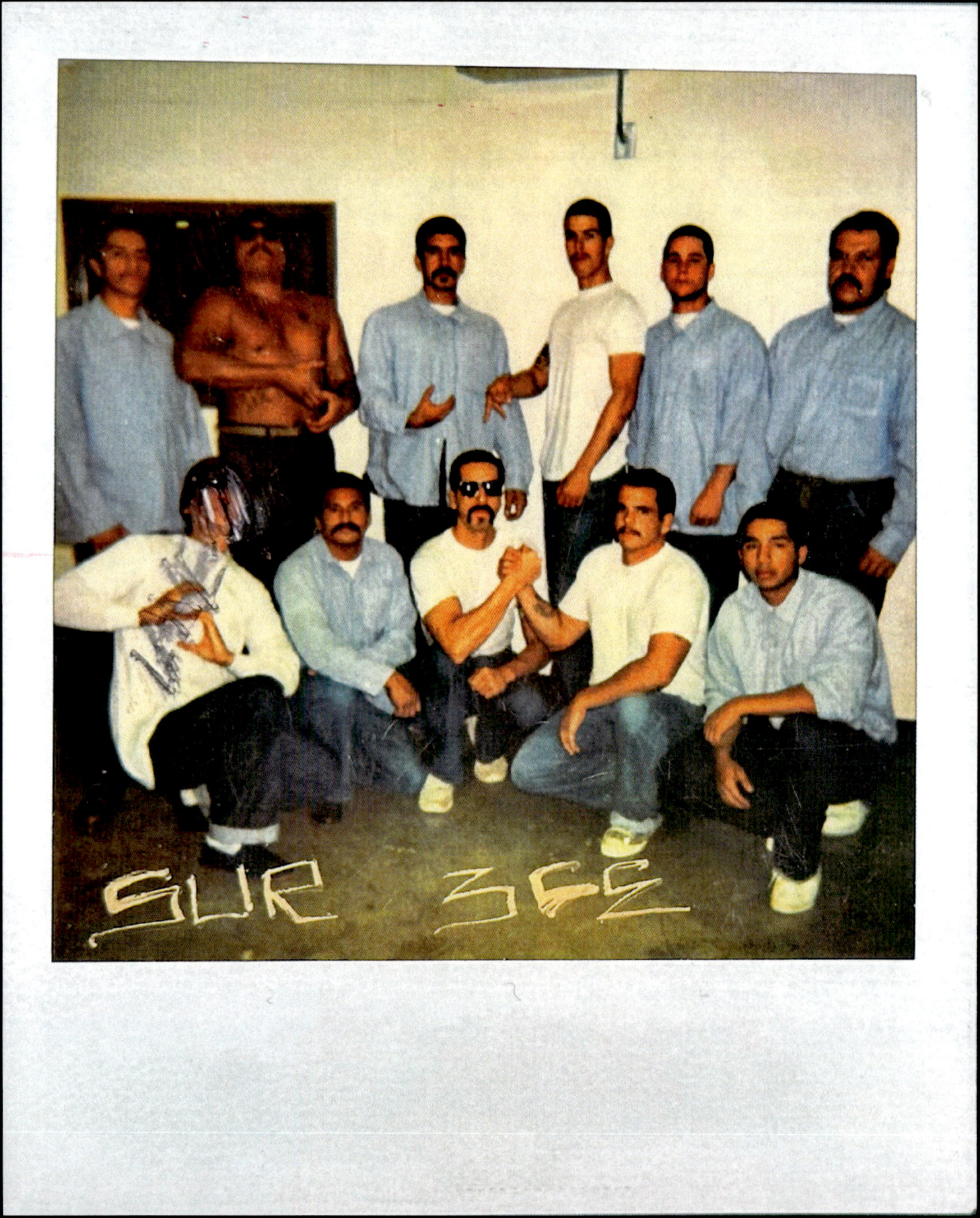

This photo of these 11 Southerners was taken in the mid-1990s at an unknown California state prison. The dude who was in this picture wrote "Lame" over his homie on the left because he "Went Out Backwards." Going out backward means a former comrade broke the rules of his "Car" and is no longer welcome around.

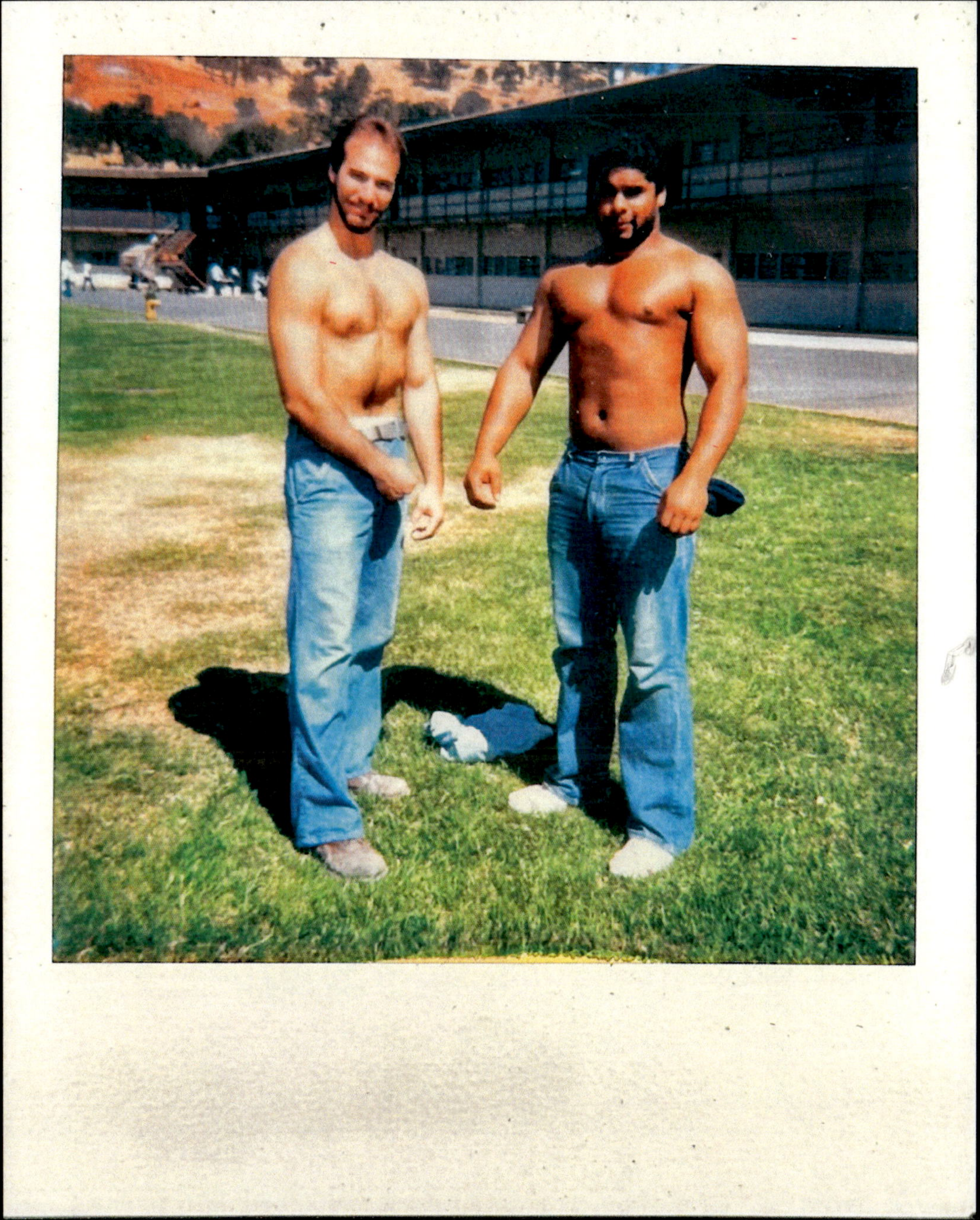

This photo was taken at Sierra Conservation Center State Prison (Jamestown) in the early 1990s. Pictured are two Peckerwoods without their shirts, showing off their physiques. Being in top physical shape is mandatory in the penitentiary. I could bench press 315 pounds for 12 repetitions when I walked the line back then.

This photo depicts several members of the Hoover Criminal Gang on a California prison yard in the mid-1990s. Five of them are throwing up the Hoover gang sign. This photo is unique because all of the inmates are lying down on the grass. Personally, I think they should have stood up for the photo because it would have looked better.

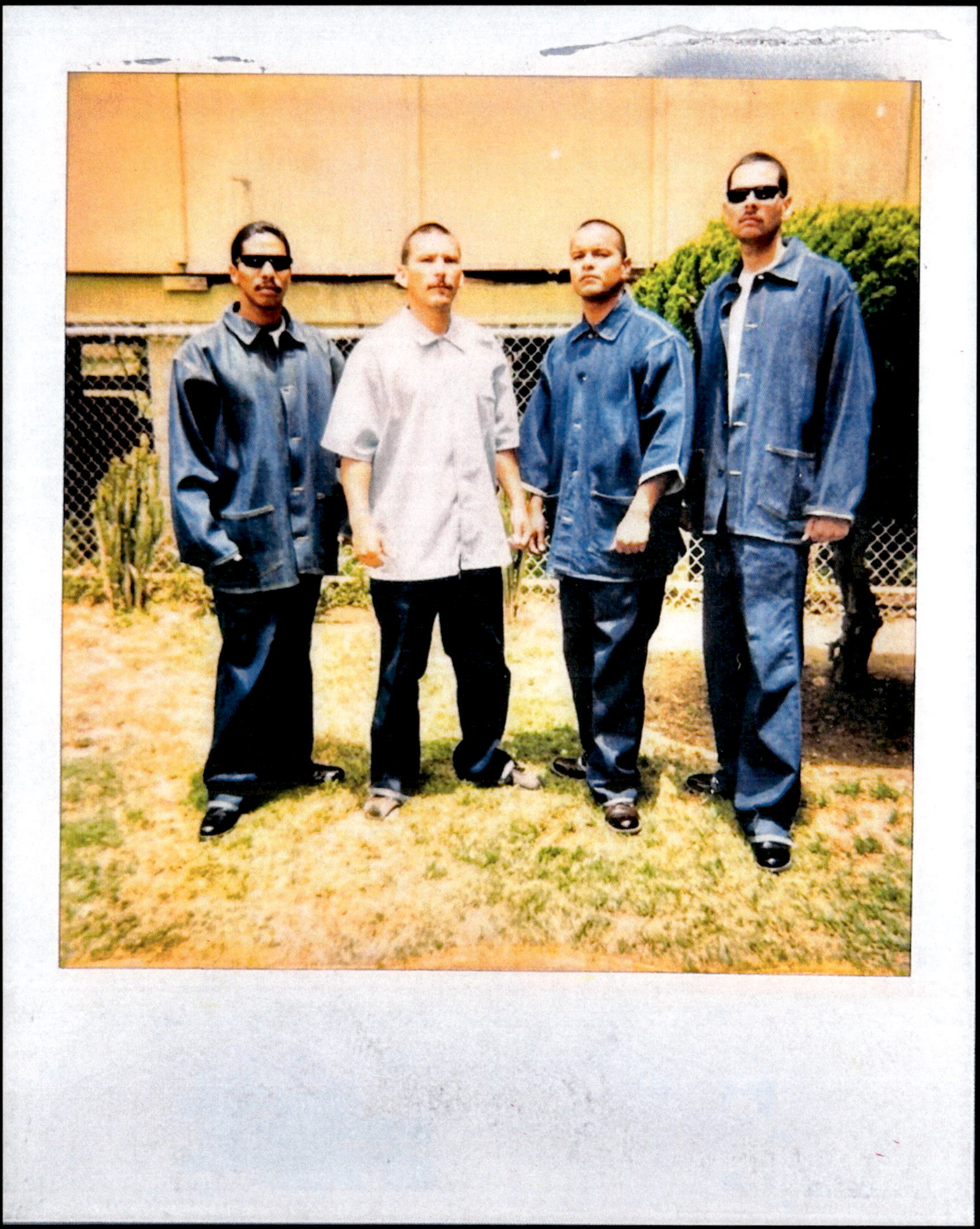

This photo of four Hispanic inmates was taken at the California Rehabilitation Center CRC, Norco) in the mid-1990s. CRC was nicknamed "Hotel California" while it was still open. Hotel California was closed in September 2026.

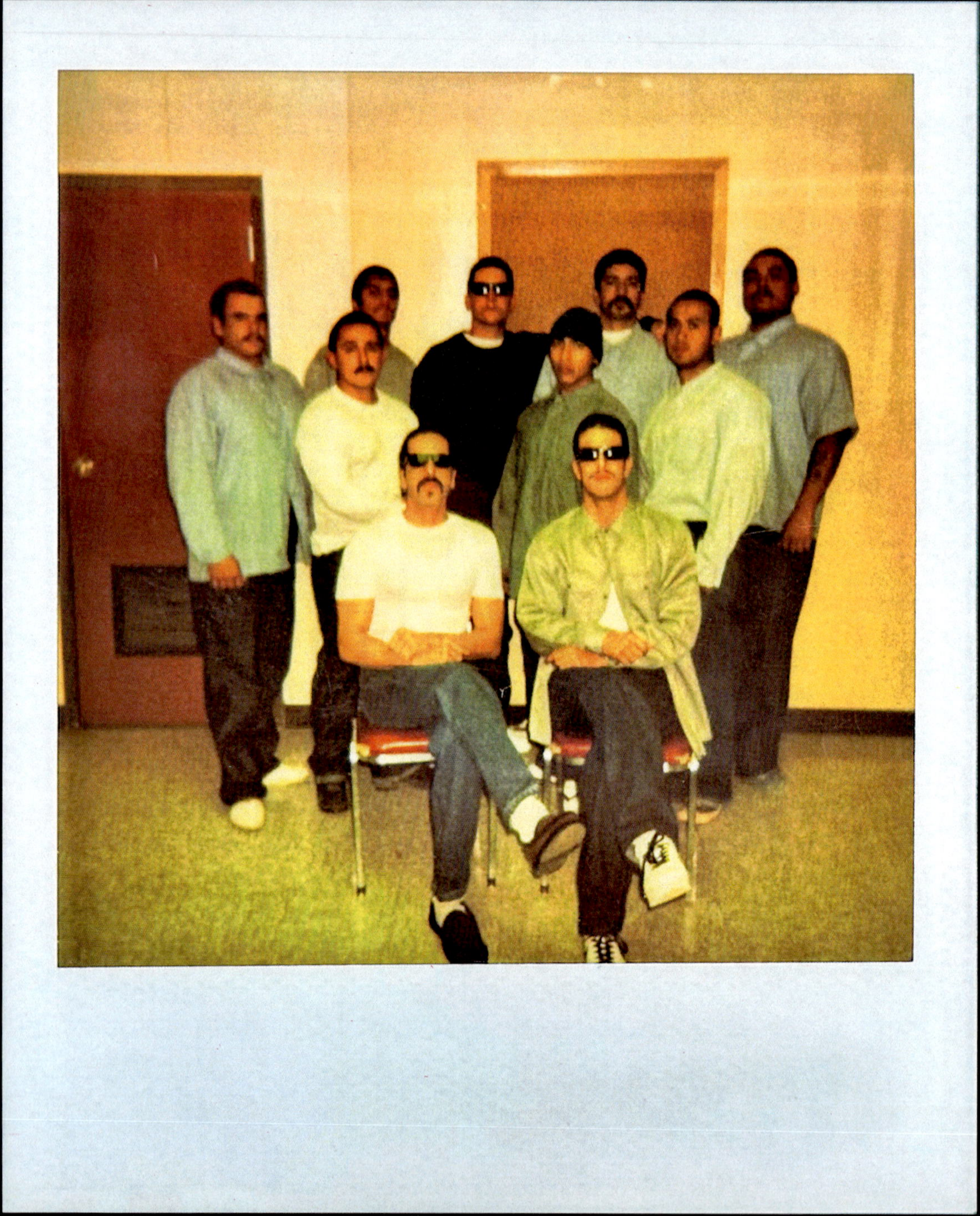

This photo, taken in the mid-1990s, depicts a group of Southerners in classic prison poses. The sitting position of the two dudes in front is something I always remembered from my years in prison. There is a variant where the inmate places his hands on the knee above in a clasped position.

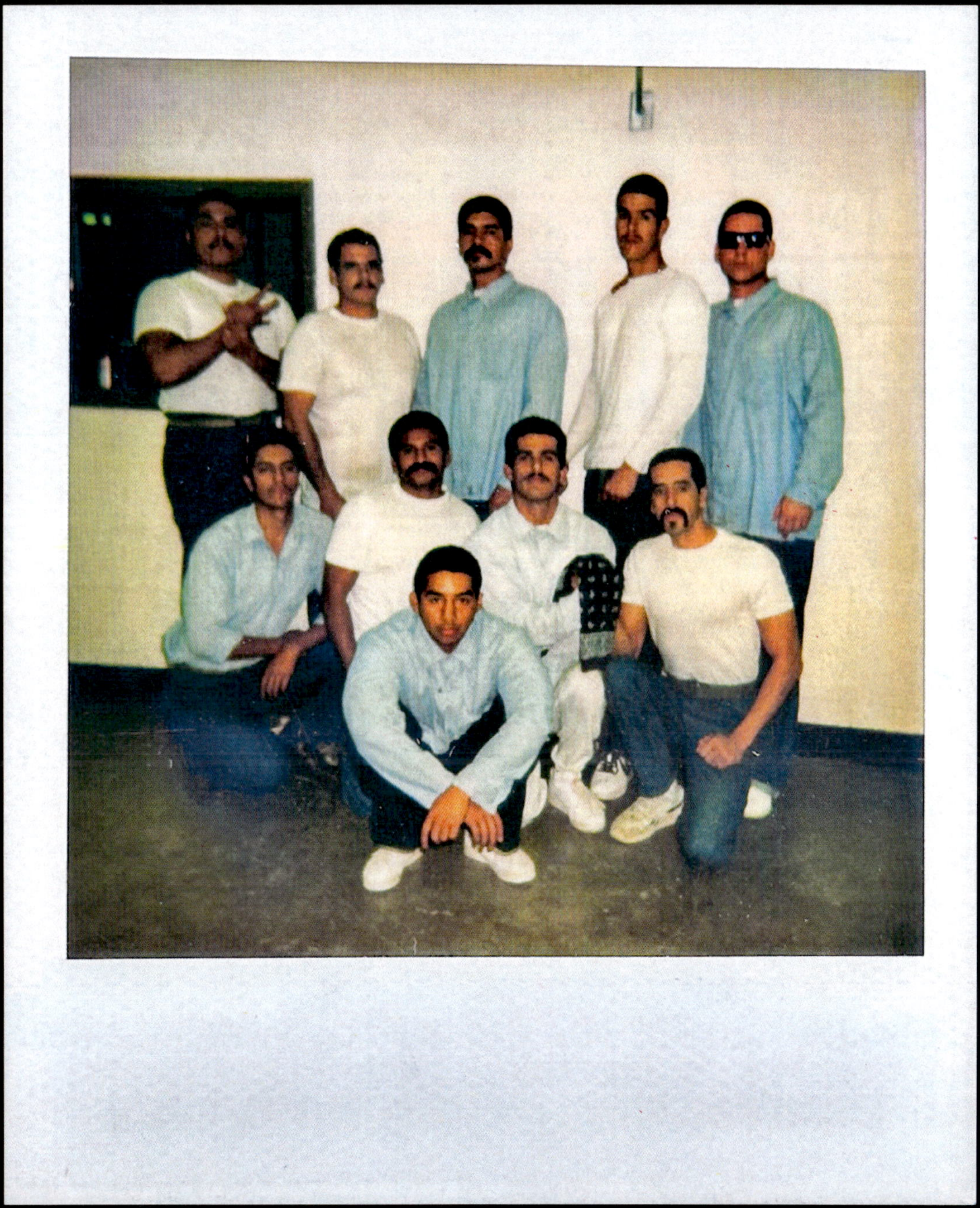

This photo of these 10 Southsiders was taken at an unknown California state prison in the mid-1990s. These pictures hold a lot of value to the convicts; the only time I really come across them is when they pass on. I was in daily contact with a young convict back in 2025, and within a few months he got sick and died. I helped his mom out with the funeral costs,

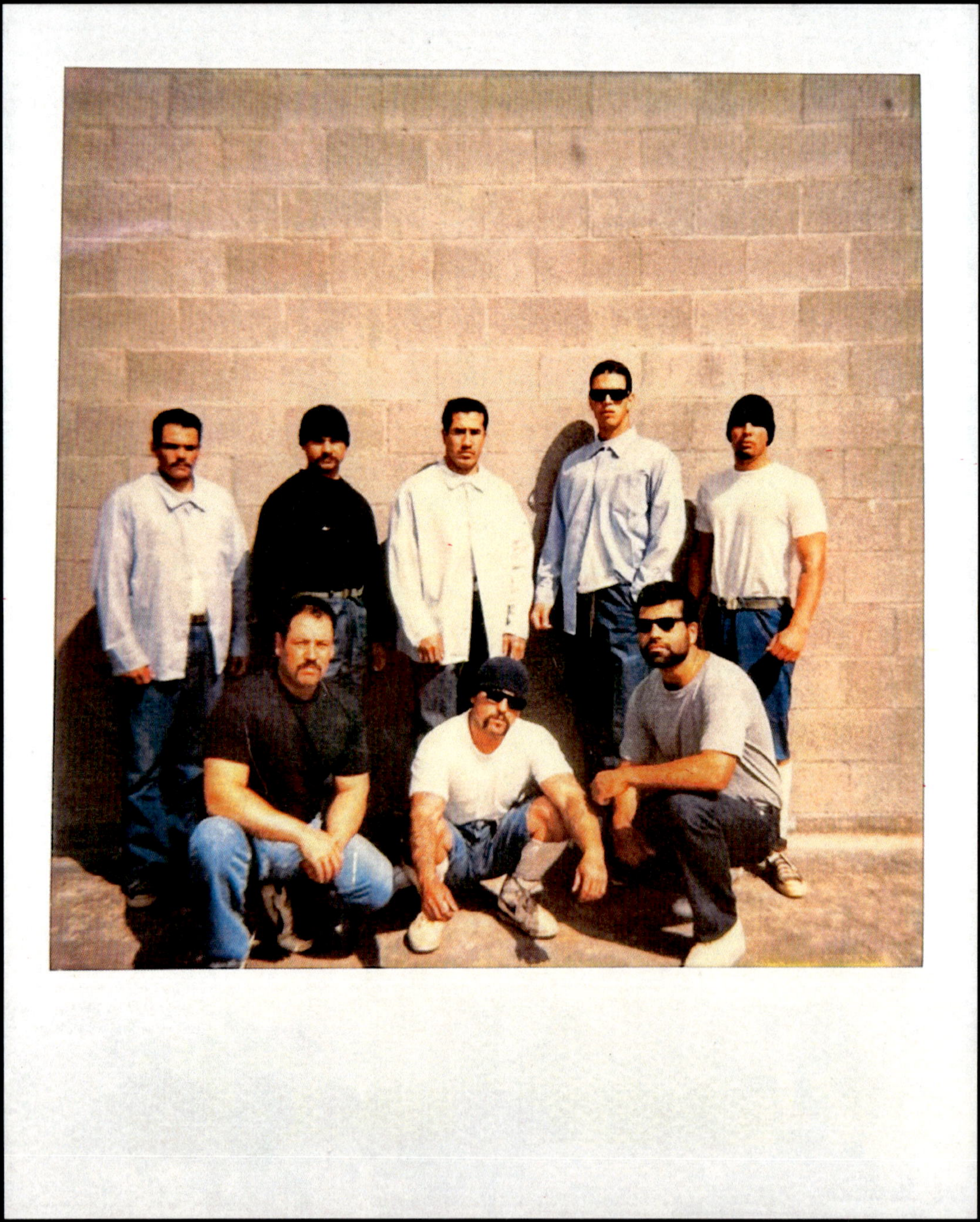

This picture was taken in the mid-1990s at an unknown California state prison. In prison photos like these with numerous inmates, the highest-ranking dude usually stands in the center of the picture. It's a respect issue, and if some low-status member tried to stand in the middle, the other dudes would tell him to kick rocks and move.

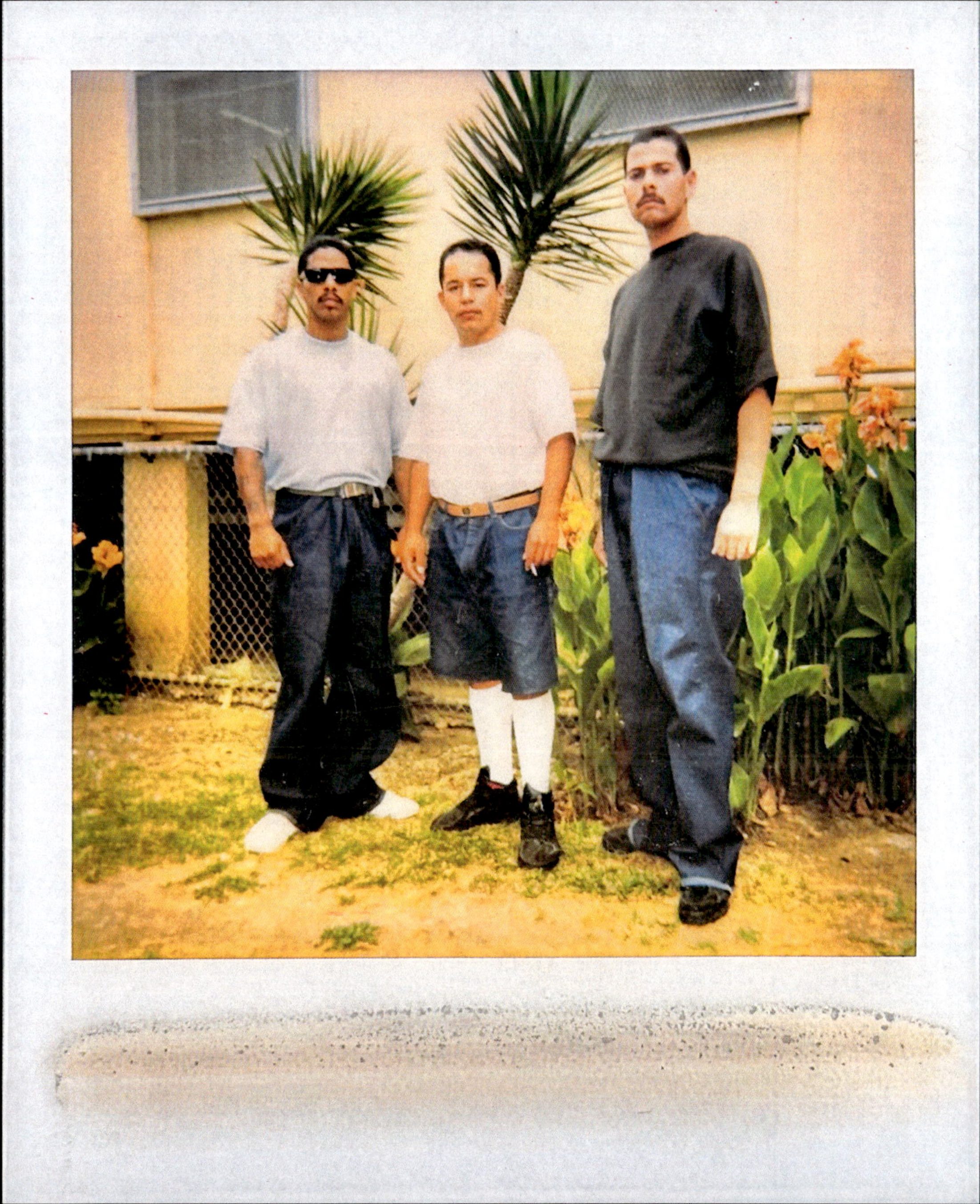

This photo, taken in the mid-1990s, depicts three Hispanic men at the California Rehabilitation Center (CRC, Norco, Hotel California). Hotel California was an iconic prison while it was open. I have heard many stories from inmates who fondly recounted their time there.

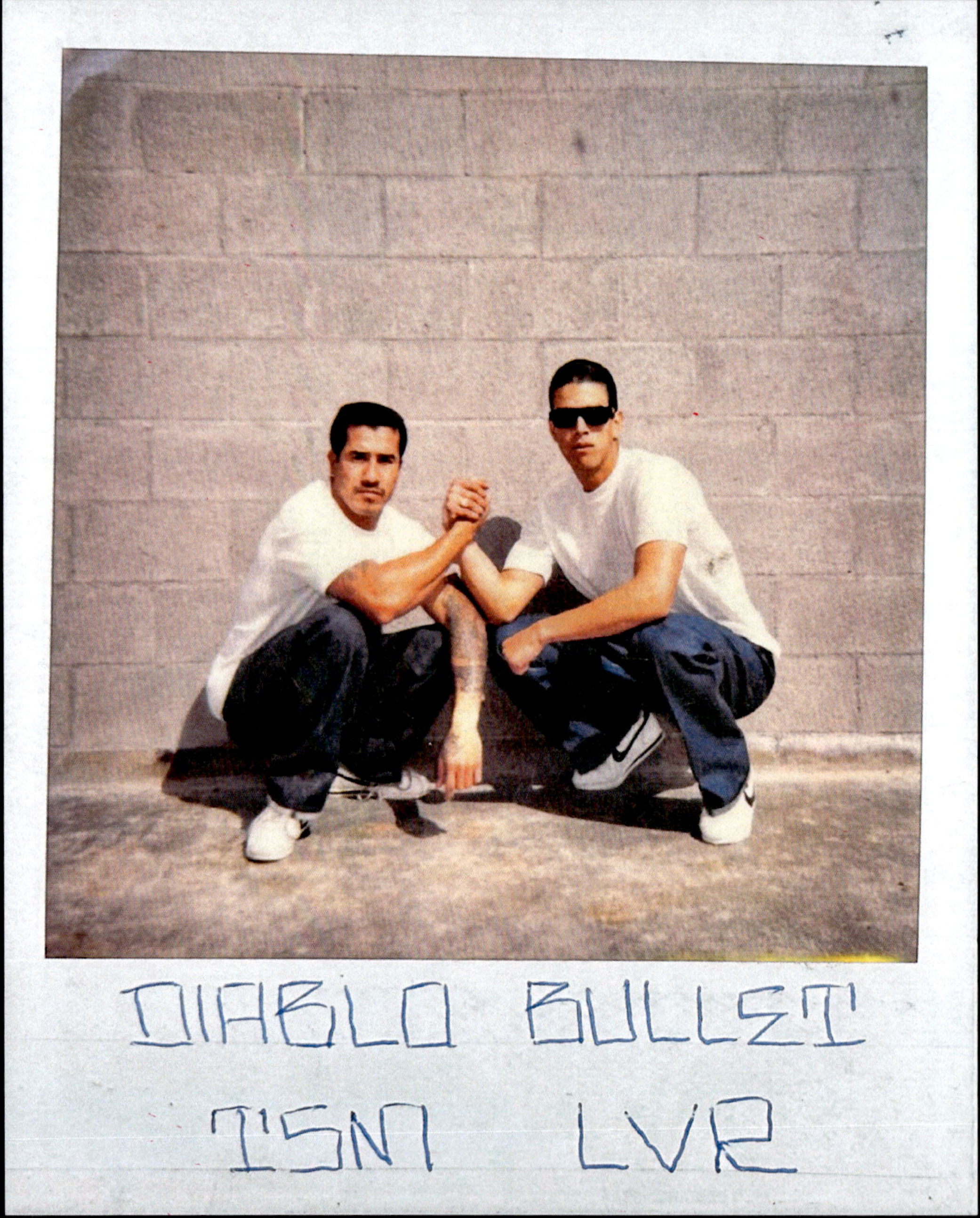

This photo, taken in the mid-1990s, depicts two Southerners in classic prison poses. Bullet and Diablo clasp their hands in a sign of solidarity on the prison yard. Bullet is a youngster, and he hasn't earned any prison ink yet. He needs to raise his hand and earn his stripes if he wants to earn respect on the yard.

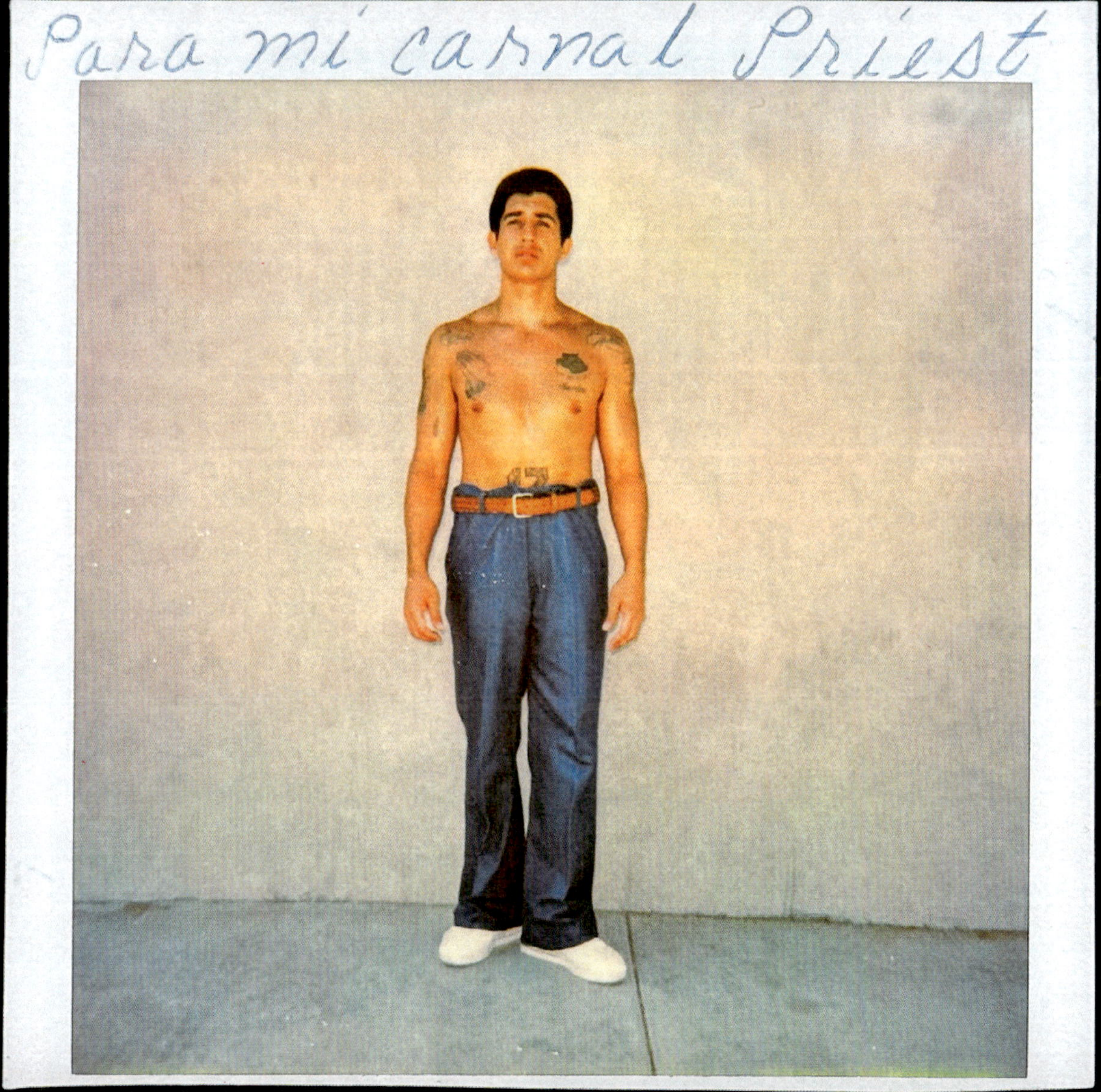

This picture of this Southsider was taken in the mid-1990s in an unknown California state prison. Every inmate needs some hustle in prison to survive and make money. I always respected the dudes who were always on the go, doing their program and making their time as comfortable as possible.

About the Author

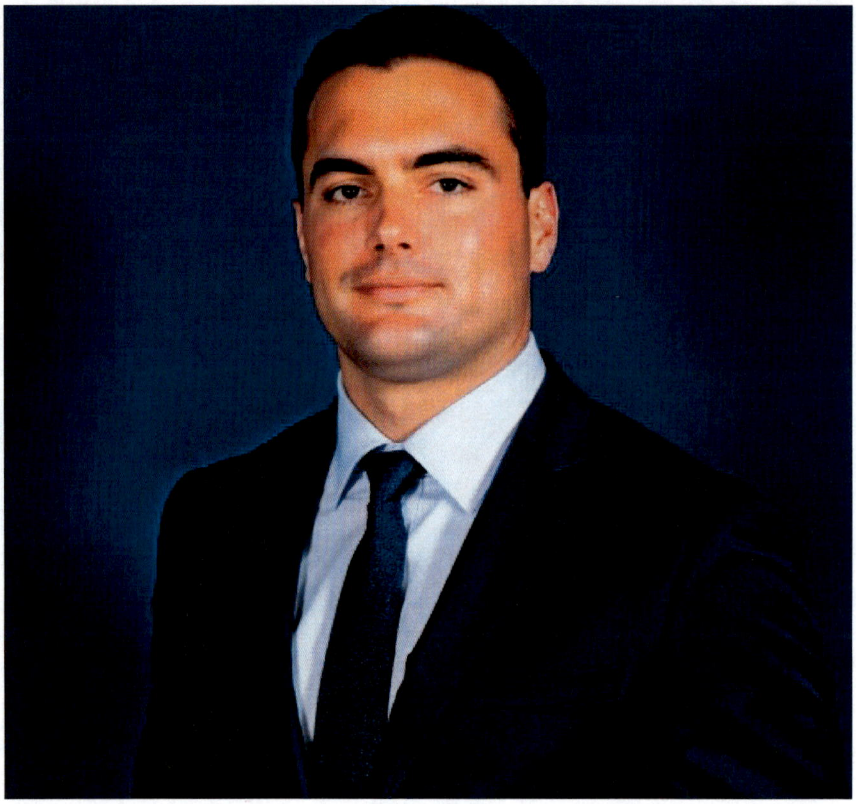

Eric enjoys the status of a dedicated husband and father, being blessed with four wonderful daughters who hold a special place in his heart. Eric's existence revolves around upholding the virtues of a devout Christian, a devoted husband, and a caring father guided by the grace of God. His journey has been transformative, considering his challenging upbringing, and he now stands as an illustrious testament to the boundless possibilities achievable through faith in God.

Eric joined a criminal street gang as a teenager, and he was eventually arrested and put in a cage at the Long Beach City Jail. He dropped out of Jordan High School in Long Beach, California, in the 10th grade. Eric eventually got on the right path by the grace of God and obtained his GED the same month that he would have graduated. He joined the United States Coast Guard at 18, and after four years of faithful service, he was honorably discharged.

The following is an excerpt from his autobiography: "California Prison Confessions." "It was a typical beautiful summer night in Long Beach, California, and the three young teens fighting in the musty garage starkly contrasted the night's serenity. A teen called Bones was thrown against a wall, and a muscular teenager nicknamed E Double (me) rushed towards him and violently punched him in his lower back. Another youth named Tim Loc held Bones against the wall during this attack. E Double's knuckles landed with a thick-sounding thud as Bones grimaced and moaned in pain from each successive blow.

There's a look of pain and fear in Bone's eyes as E Double mercilessly lands blow after blow to his kidneys. E Double has spent years hitting the heavy bag in his garage, so his punches are devastating for his age. The beating lasted a minute, and the two teens stopped attacking the unfortunate victim. Amazingly, they all shook hands and embraced each other. We were all friends, and this was our modest gang initiation into our small clique called 'Six Feet Under.'"

Our tiny neighborhood gang in North Long Beach, California, had several members of various races: White, Black, and Hispanic. The definition of a criminal street gang according to the California Penal Code is as follows: "As used in this chapter, 'criminal street gang' means any ongoing organization, association, or group of three or more persons, whether formal or informal, having as one of its primary activities the commission of one or more of the criminal acts…having a common name or common identifying sign or symbol, and whose members individually or collectively engage in or have engaged in a pattern of criminal gang activity," California Penal Code 186.22(f).

Some of our associates committed serious crimes such as burglaries, drug sales, stealing cars, carrying guns, vandalism, and assaulting people. Although we were nothing but young punks, we were a criminal street gang according to the California Penal Code.

The FBI did a study entitled "Street-Gang Mentality: A Mosaic of Remorseless Violence and Relentless Loyalty." I want to quote a relevant part concerning young males who do not have a father or other positive male role models in their lives while growing up: "All gang members lacked male role models in their households, and when they lived with their mothers, they were rarely home because of work schedules. Gang members often lived temporarily with various people. All but one gang member reported that one or more immediate family members had a criminal history or abused drugs. Gangs attracted them because of their loyalty, stability, and sense of group identity."

There is an epidemic in this country of boys masquerading as men who don't take their responsibilities as fathers seriously. Many fathers aren't involved in their children's lives; if they are, they are a horrible example of what a real man should be. One of the main factors in young men ending up in the penal system is the lack of a father or, at the very least, a positive male role model when they were growing up. Absentee fathers are causing society to pay a high price for their selfish and callous actions.

Every day, I strive to be the best dad to the four beautiful daughters God has blessed me with. I live by the motto, "Be the man you needed as a child." I will not allow the actions of physically and emotionally abusive people to define who I am or hinder my advancement in life. You can choose to be bitter or better. I strive for excellence because living well is the best response to abusive people.

Eric Sturgess

God bless you and yours.

Romans 10:9-13

For those seeking to connect with Eric or gather additional insights about his upcoming projects, please visit his official website: EricSturgess.com.

Other Books

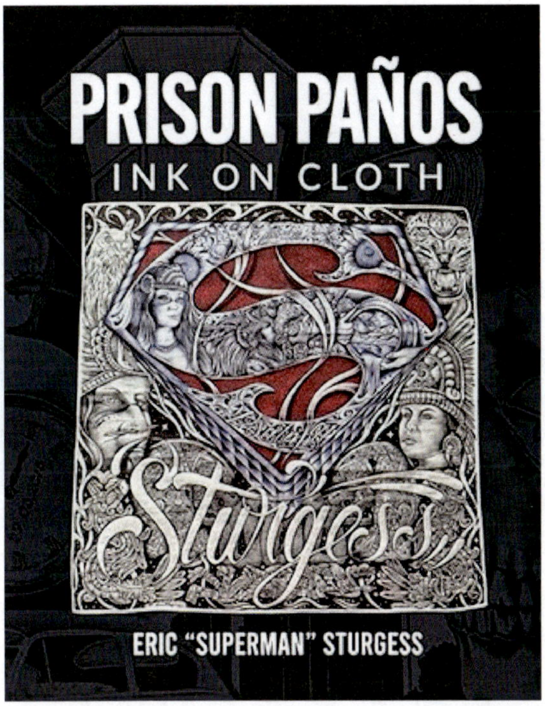

Prison Paños: Ink On Cloth

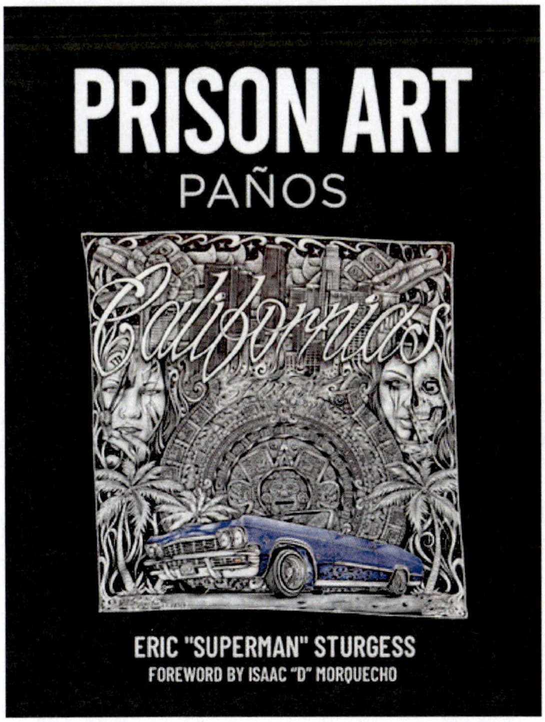

Prison Art Paños

Prison Art Hats

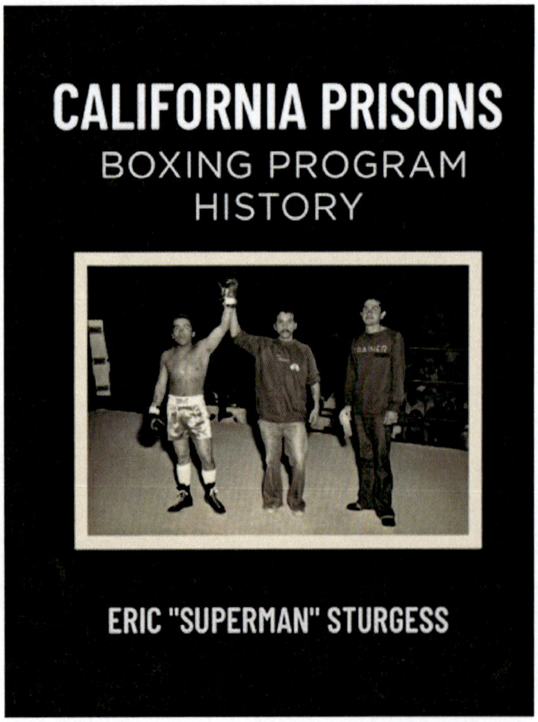

California Prisons:
Boxing Program History

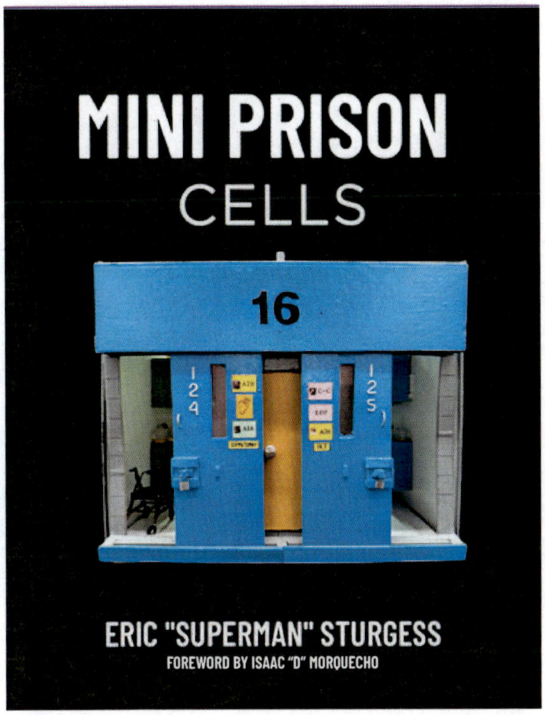

Mini Prison Cells

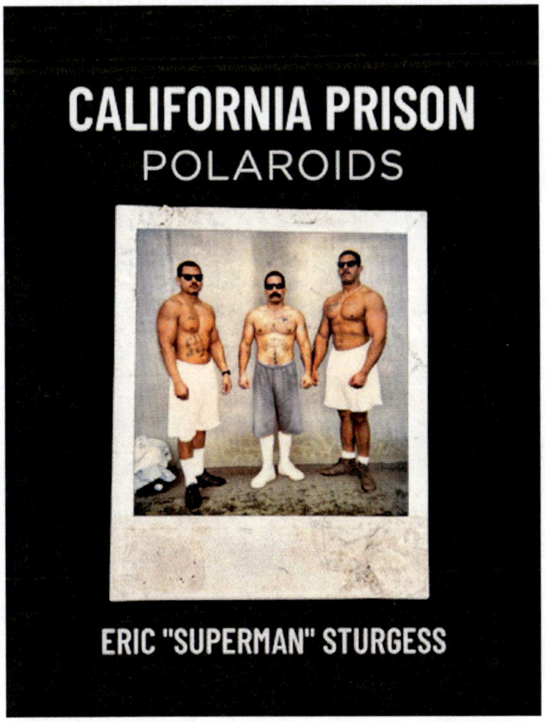

California Prison Polaroids

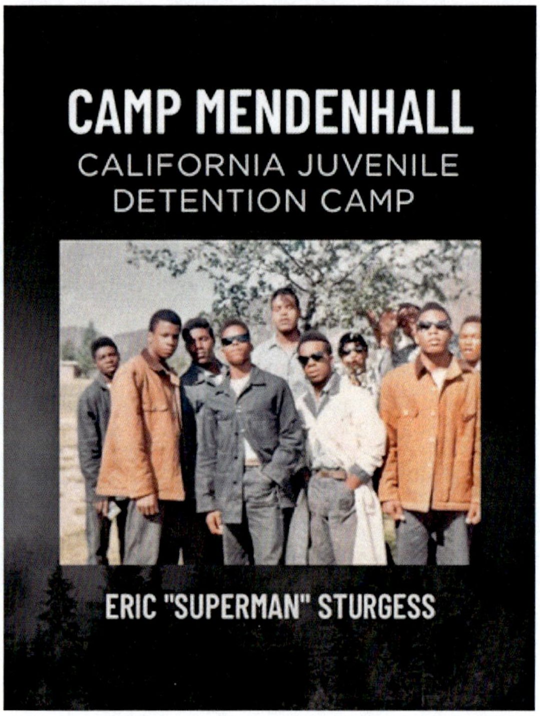

Camp Mendenhall: California Juvenile Detention Camp

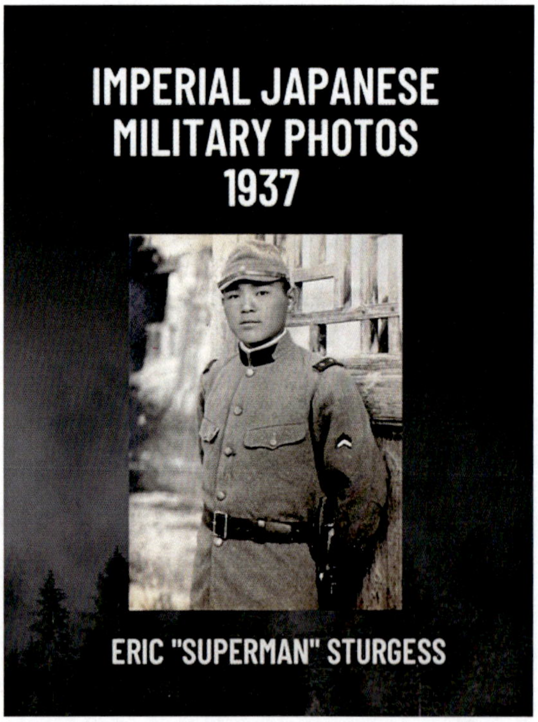

Imperial Japanese Military Photos 1937

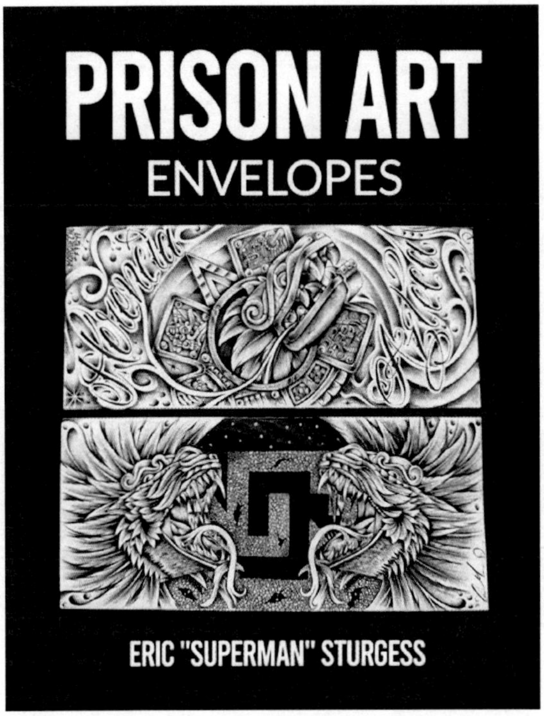

Prison Art Envelopes

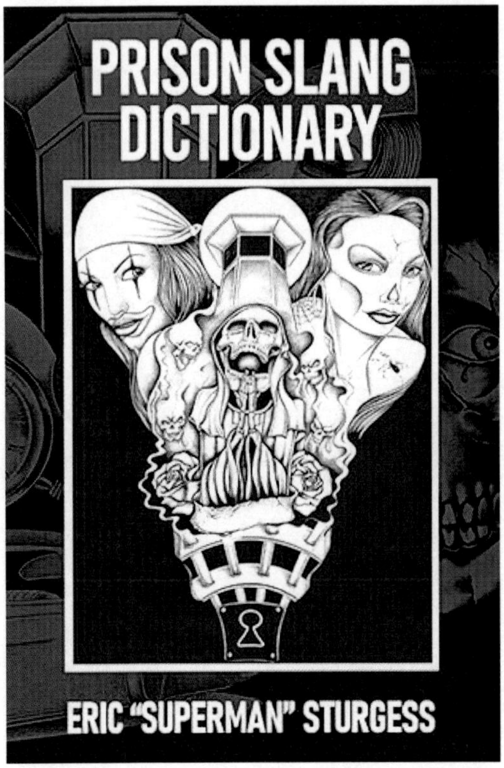

Prison Slang Dictionary

Made in United States
North Haven, CT
05 November 2026

21765355R00024